YOUR
GUARDIAN
ANGEL

Claire Nahmad has published a number of books on healing, herbalism, magic and folklore. She lives in South Yorkshire, England.

By the Same Author

Love Spells

Cat Spells

Garden Spells

Dream Spells

Fairy Spells

Earth Magic

Magical Animals

The Enchanted Garden

The Cat Herbal

The Book of Peace

The Fairy Pack

Summoning Angels

The Secret Teachings of Mary Magdalene (With Margaret Bailey)

YOUR GUARDIAN ANGEL

CONNECT, COMMUNICATE, AND HEAL
WITH YOUR OWN DIVINE COMPANION

CLAIRE NAHMAD

WATKINS PUBLISHING
LONDON

Distributed in the USA and Canada by Sterling Publishing Co., Inc.
387 Park Avenue South, New York, NY 10016

This edition published in the UK and USA 2007 by
Watkins Publishing, Sixth Floor, Castle House,
75–76 Wells Street, London W1T 3QH

Designed and typeset by Jerry Goldie

Printed in the U.S.A

ISBN 13: 978-1-84293-142-4

For Dianne Pegler,
in memory of past times

ACKNOWLEDGEMENTS

Acknowledgements are due to the White Eagle Lodge, London (tel. +44 [0] 20 7603 7914) for their kind permission to quote material from publications by White Eagle; to Virginia Essene and Irving Feurst for the many illuminations I have gained from their spiritual studies and writings; and to Margaret Bailey for kindly permitting me to quote material from our book, *The Secret Teachings of Mary Magdalene*.

CONTENTS

INTRODUCTION

This book focuses particularly on the guardian angel. Many people speak of such allies in terms of an angelic group, or believe that a relative who has passed over has become their guardian angel. Whilst such human spirits assuredly do work with the guardian angel to offer protection to a loved one, I believe that the guardian angel is not human, or one of a group of angels, but that it is a single entity belonging to each individual human being. It reflects our guide, an advanced human spirit who is allied to every soul coming into incarnation on earth. Each of us has many guides and many angels in attendance as we walk our path through life, but these two, the main guide and the guardian angel allotted to every human being, are the two supreme sources of guidance and guardianship – the guardian angel at our left-hand side, and the guide at our right.

The purpose of this book is to help readers to develop their relationship with their guardian angel through ritual, prayer, various methods of attunement, and direct experience. The guardian angel has a huge part to play in the field of relationships – relationships with other human beings, with the world of nature, and, ultimately, with our divine source. Perhaps the most important relationship of all, one which needs our special care and attention, and, almost invariably, very hard work, is our relationship with ourselves! This is where the help and inspiration of the guardian angel, and the unique light it can throw into dark and denied places, comes into its own.

Life lived in conscious communion with our guardian angel is a life enriched and enhanced beyond measure. However, we do need to build our relationship with our guardian. Some people believe that we come into incarnation with this relationship already in place, but in my experience this is not so. A fundamental relationship already exists, but it is an unconscious one. It is a part of the purpose of human life on earth to develop a conscious relationship with our guardian angel, so earthing the divine into common experience, and thus transforming our lives and our destiny, on both an individual and a global scale.

I would like to describe how I see my own guardian angel. It appears in beautiful swathes of colour above my bed each night. It has fields of energy that both look and waft like great wings hovering over me. Its colours are always the same, but if I happen to be working on a certain problem or project, other colours sometimes occur. If it doesn't come, I call it or 'summon' it, and thereafter it appears. Its main colour is amethyst deepening into violet, and I often catch a glimpse of that colour (emanating from an incorporeal source) during the day. This is my sign that my guardian angel is responding to my conscious awareness of its presence. The strangest thing about my guardian angel is that I can study it closely with my physical eyes, but, if I close them, I continue to see the angel just as well!

One of the many magical and poetic aspects of angel communication is that their language is a language of colour. They speak to us, not only in words and in symbols, but especially in colours, communing with us through every differing hue. Angelic colours always shine with a wondrous diamond clarity, radiant and transparent as if they are lit by an inner light – they are never muddy, brash or heavy.

As your relationship with your own guardian angel develops, you will become aware of its colour or colours, and these will give an indication of what your angel is saying to you – its great theme and plan for your life – entrusted to it by your higher self, your spiritual aspect that never leaves the supernal worlds and that is in perfect accord with your angel. This, in turn, points to the colour ray to which you are attuned, which develops the message further. Each one of us comes into being under the influence of one or more of the seven great rays of creation, whose essence and mystery are reflected in the lovely and ethereal manifestation of the rainbow.

Summoning the Awen

The ancient Druids spoke of the mystical 'Awen', the vast spiritual ocean of inspiration from which humankind draws the inner essence which becomes poetry, song, prophecy, every branch of science and medicine and every artistic discipline, true religion and law. The Awen is the angelic realm, and it is within the great Awen that our guardian angel rests, ready to serve, protect, commune with and inspire us as soon as we sound the note that summons it. One of the simplest means of signalling to our angel that we are ready to receive its gifts is just to chant the word 'Awen' itself. Draw out each vowel sound to a count of five, and allow a slight tremolo vibration to run through your enunciation of the word. Become aware of the strong and clear connection to the earth and to the angelic worlds that the uttering of this magical word gives you. Do this in the knowledge that you are linking with your guardian angel, and feel those links of light forming a channel to receive your intentional communion. Then your conscious relationship with your angel can begin.

CHAPTER ONE

THE GUARDIAN ANGEL

I had offered the refuge of my home to a man who had just been released from prison. Unknown to me at the time, the prison in which he had been incarcerated was one of the most notorious in Europe, and ran a brutal regime. He had been confined in one of its cells for several years, and as the days passed, it became increasingly clear that this man had both witnessed and participated in such extremes of experience that he had become dangerously unstable, if not psychopathic. To make matters even more unsettling and eerie, his mental balance deserted him as darkness fell each evening, returning gradually after dawn. This meant that sleep during the night was usually impossible; and after a week or two of this harrowing routine, I began to feel that my own sanity was becoming somewhat blurred around the edges. One night, events reached a climax. He grabbed the curtains and tried to set them on fire with his cigarette lighter, announcing that it was our destiny to die together in the flames. It was at this point that I put out a silent call to my guardian angel to come to my aid.

Shortly afterwards, his mood changed and his attitude became more normal. He was able to set out on a long healing journey from that point (necessarily, away from my home!) which culminated in a desire to help others trapped in similarly dark places of the soul. The incident I have described was so dramatic, traumatic and transformative that I would like to try to explain what I sensed actually took place after I made my call to my guardian angel.

First of all, I was given instantly an inner reassurance that I was not alone, and that all would be well. Secondly, I received an

intimation that the situation was very delicately balanced, and that
to bring it to a conclusion without either of us suffering serious
injury would require absolute cooperation on my part. This cooperation consisted of remaining quiet and collected, taking no action or
decision of my own, and waiting for the promptings of my guardian
angel. Thirdly, I became aware that my angel called on the spirit of
the beautiful pine tree that stood outside the window, and that both
angel and tree-spirit conjoined to create a stabilizing and protective energy field around my dangerous predicament. This seemed
to have three main functions: to prevent further escalation of the
disruption; to ground and calm us both with energies from the wise,
strong, serene, sane Earth; and to introduce the cleansing and loving
influences from the tree-spirit right into the tumultuous heart of
the situation, where they combined with those of my angel to
soothe the jagged, lightning-like, dangerous dynamics in expression
all around us. As this was achieved, the angel and the tree-spirit
together instantaneously began to build a new, purer atmosphere of
reassuring normality in which wholesome human responses could
flourish. I then became aware that my disturbed friend's guardian
angel was lending its strength and support to the entire operation,
although its aid was not fully able to manifest until he had begun to
calm down.

All of this took place immediately and simultaneously. It con-
firmed my half-formed belief that the guardian angel does indeed
summon others of its kin to rectify a threatening situation, and, fur-
thermore, calls on etheric beings (such as the tree-spirit) to lend
their aid as well. In other words, the guardian angel networks!

The Language of Nature

Since that time, I have become increasingly aware that the guardian
angel summons natural creatures, and also signs and messages from
the elements themselves, to help, guide and comfort us. A cloud
might take shape in the form of a symbol, to inspire or guide us.
Animals, insects and birds might bring themselves to our attention
(particularly birds, who share a beautiful affinity with angels and

who link us to them quite naturally via their song and configurations of flight* to convey a blessing from our guardian angel.

It is worth studying the language of the natural world. Let folklore, myth, legend and fairy tale teach you the intriguing meanings associated with its animate and inanimate manifestations, that rich vernacular which has made itself known to human consciousness since the beginning of time. Don't be inhibited in adding your own interpretations. For instance, wasps seem to like me a lot! Folklore associates them with warnings of spiteful gossip, but in fact I feel no negative emanation from them. They purposely seek me out, and a queen or two invariably finds her way into my house in the spring. They never attack; and I have come to associate them with the fact that they taught humankind how to make paper. Their nests of pulped wood or papier-mâché were what first inspired us to create writing and printing material from the soft pulp of wood. Wasps are also very industrious creatures, and wear symbolic black and gold (light and darkness working together to bring forth creation); so whenever I am visited by them, I know that it is time to start work on another writing project!

There is a wonderful 'lost' chapter in *Alice In Wonderland* about a grumpy but good-hearted wasp ('The Wasp In a Wig'), and I agree with Lewis Carroll that wasps are to be regarded as ancient in spirit, venerable, and secretly amiable!

In his book on his travels throughout Romania and Hungary (*Raggle-taggle*), the English professor and author, Walter Starkie, describes a fascinating incident. On a beautiful moonlit summer's night (he describes the country round about as 'looking like fairyland' under its rays) he stopped by a knoll, upon which 'a small rustic graveyard nestled peacefully', to make his camp. As he lit a fire and sat by it, he was filled with an overwhelming feeling of sorrow, loneliness, vulnerability and apprehension (his first warning from his intuition, fostered by his guardian angel, that something was amiss). Determined not to be 'superstitious' and to shrug these feelings off, he settled down to sleep. However, as soon as the fire

*See my book, Summoning Angels, which gives a comprehensive overview of this subject.

burnt low, he was invaded by a marauding company of mosquitoes 'and every other species of stinging insect' (his second warning) which made sleep impossible. Protecting himself from these tormentors, he tried to sleep again. This time, insects of every kind, from earwigs, beetles and woodlice to, finally, a legion of ants, did their utmost to try to keep him awake. Still he failed to heed their warning! At last, he did drop off to sleep for a short while, only to be woken by a yelping dog at his side. The dog belonged to an extraordinary little, wizened man, 'like one of the goblins in Grimm's fairy tales… His long white beard nearly touched the ground' and 'he seemed to be clothed in a garment of reeds mixed with the plumage of birds.'

This strange, fairy-like being sat with him and told him stories of the unbenign spirits that were known to haunt this particular graveyard, who attacked at the astral level when their victims were sleeping. The little man kept him company until dawn, recounting his tales until first light, and introducing a strange shrieking sound into his voice whenever the professor started to nod off, which immediately reawakened him. As the sun rose, the strange little old man led him out of the graveyard, careful not to take his leave until he had seen Starkie safely on his way.

In recounting this remarkable incident, the author clearly does not recognize the presence of his guardian angel throughout that night, and the kindly aid it has called forth from the insect and animal world (one is tempted to say, also, the fairy world, except that the intriguing little old man did appear to have a mortal existence, although some readers might feel that this was questionable!). He does not even seem to have realized that he was most certainly (I believe) in danger from hostile entities, although he does remark…'the old man's superstitious nature had already infected me and I felt that all this experience had something supernatural about it'. Perhaps this last comment reveals the prevalence of the materialist viewpoint, which is ever blind to the care and guardianship our angel can give us.

A well-known message from the insect world pertains to the presence of fairies. Whenever a certain place is rich in fairy life, our guardian angel will call our attention to it, for our own delight and benefit (because the fairy energies are ever healing and inspiring for our earth-tired psyches). It does this by calling on the aid of lady-birds, who will land on us, or on a plant near to us, generally catching our attention by their behaviour. I had believed that it was only myself whose attention was thus alerted to the fairies by the presence of ladybirds, but so many people have reported similar experiences that I have had to desert such fond suppositions!

Angelic Intervention

The incident of the disturbed man in my house shows, I hope, how easy it is to call on your guardian angel for help, and the dramatic and transforming effect its aid can bring. Its intervention assumes stages that can be set out in three steps:

- The guardian angel responds instantly to your call for help by imparting to you a feeling of reassurance.
- It asks for your cooperation, and for your willingness to turn the entire situation over to your angel. If an office-worker is delegated a task, it becomes impossible to perform if the delegator hangs over the worker's shoulder, fussing and interfering and virtually doing the work herself. Give your angel permission to be entirely in command.
- The angel asks for confirmation of your wholehearted trust.

Consciously cooperating with these three steps will facilitate your angel's ability to serve you in crises. Your angel's instructions will come to you through your own conscious thought-processes. You will be aware that you are subtly listening and cooperating, rather than asserting your own self-will. It is really a matter of allowing the personality to sink into temporary abeyance.

An important lesson for me to draw from my experience, of course, was one which is best described by the adage 'Fools rush in where angels fear to tread'. The spiritual teacher White Eagle advises us that, if we have important work to do for the benefit of others, our guardian angel will always afford us protection, no matter what the circumstances. He further advises, however, that this assurance needs to be finely balanced with a responsible awareness of unnecessary risk-taking. It is very easy to mistake a naïve arrogance for absolute trust in angelic protection. We may enjoy such trust, but we need to assess the risks we might take with humility and responsibility, without falling into the egotistical trap of thinking: 'Nothing could possibly hurt me, whatever I do.'

Christ's temptation in the desert, where the Adversary urged him to hurl himself from the mountainside in order to prove that the angels would spectacularly come to his rescue, reflects this soul lesson that each of us has to incorporate into our fund of wisdom.

The Sword of Michael

Another method of overcoming fear through wisdom and discretion is taught to us by our guardian angel. Our angel appears to us in dreams, shrouded in darkness. It seems to be a figure in a nightmare. Yet, if we master our fear and panic, and make a conscious decision to trust, to say deep within ourselves 'This is Goddess/God's world' – so rejecting the illusion of fear, darkness and evil – the dark cloak falls away to reveal the radiant being within. This lesson is crucial, because if we fail to learn it, the God-given dynamics within our deeper being help to create, not the paradise on earth that is the master plan of creation, but the world of chaos, injustice, fear and suffering that is so prevalent today.

Those who work with angels are called upon to wield the mighty sword within – Archangel Michael's sword – which cuts through the apparently gargantuan powers of illusion and delivers us into the world of truth – the world of Goddess/God. We can only achieve this by stoically refusing to lease our being (be-lieving) to the illusory realms of fear and horror that are always trying to claim us for their own and are ever eager to precipitate us into tangible expressions of their principalities. Our guardian angels long to securely set the power of the Sword of Michael in our hands so that we become dynamos of the true creative impulse. When we thus resonate with the Divine, we become builders of the temple that will one day (not necessarily so far off as we think!) be raised over all the Earth, so that all her creatures, from the least to the greatest, will live in happiness and without oppression within the encirclement of the blessing and protection of the Great Mother, the sentient Earth.

It might appear to be a contradiction in terms that our guardian angel seems to try to frighten us! But, of course, the fear it evokes in us when it manifests in its dark guise is not implanted by the angel. The fear itself is an impostor, and needs to be driven out, because its intention is to deprive us of our true birthright, which is the realization of ourselves as free spiritual beings interacting in harmony with one another and with all creatures. Teaching us to overcome our fear is an act of mercy initiated by our guardian angel's deep and flawless love for us. Throughout our lesson, we are held in the strength and security of that deep and flawless love. It is the safest way imaginable to face and master the challenge of fear, humankind's greatest enemy.

Our Greatest Gift

It is important to remember that our guardian angel wholly respects our free will. When we want help and guidance, we have to ask for it, deliberately, directly, and clearly. The guardian angel will never override that most precious gift given to us as entities of ascending consciousness – our freewill choice. If we do not request the help and guidance of our guardian angel, its ability to protect us is drastically circumscribed. Fortunately, most of us do at least call on our angel subconsciously, so it is able to provide some measure of protection.

Because the guardian angel affords our gift of free will absolute respect, the 'handle of the door is on our side'. It is vital to remember this point. We must initiate and invite contact, and consciously use that handle to throw open the door on the angelic worlds, which are ours to experience once we are willing to be received into them.

Angel Visualizations

Sometimes, from our own human perspective, a simple call to our angel is not enough for us to realize that our summons actually has opened the door. We can be certain that our guardian angel will never fail us, that the faithful response to our call for help, comfort or protection will come; but we may not be able to feel the presence of our angel, or any awareness of the angelic realms. I would like to offer four little visualizations that I have often used when my deeper perception seems to have closed down, and a measure of distraction or agitation has prevented any attunement to the magical spheres where angels dwell. When using them, just breathe a little more deeply and easily, focusing on nothing but the rhythm of the breath for a moment or two; then choose one of the visualizations, according to whichever element (earth, water, air or fire) appeals to you most at the time.

Star-Visualizations of the Elements

To Still Your Mind and Emotions and Lead You to Your Heart-Centre

Fire

Create the perfect form of a six-pointed star shining above your head. Connect with it via your heart-centre. Just sit in peace, gazing into the heart of the star, feeling its stillness and the beauty of its radiance. Bathe in its profuse and endless light.

Now see an angel coming towards you. It is your guardian angel, bearing a mystical flame to bless you and to light your way; and bringing a gift to your heart, according to your need, to heal whatever it is that disturbs you.

Water

Sit in stillness under the star, as before, and see the beautiful angel coming towards you, your own guardian angel. It gives you a magical experience. Taking your hand, it leads you towards a mighty angelic being robed in the soft blue of summer skies, with great wings as white as swansdown. You actually walk through this immense angel. The feeling is as if you are floating in a great, hushed, warm ocean, tenderly being washed by gentle sighing tides of endless peace, deep as eternity; for this is indeed an Angel of Peace, and with her holy peace she deeply blesses you. Your guardian angel has never left your side, and in its arms you quietly reach the shore of this great ocean of tranquillity, and step through a golden gateway into your shining heart-centre.

There your angel awaits, holding a crystal cup of water so bright and clear and dancing that it is as if an eternal stream of diamonds cascades from its surface. The angel bids you drink, and places the cup in your hands. As you imbibe this sacred water, you drink in the essence of the angelic qualities you most need and long for.

Earth

Sit in quietude beneath the peacefully shining star, feeling the gentle inflow and outflow of your breathing. Your guardian angel appears within the star and comes towards you. Taking your hand, it leads you into the very heart of the star, where you find an exquisite garden of the spirit which encompasses you with sweetness and fragrance.

Rest awhile in this magical garden, surrounded by the beauty and the peace of nature. See your angel as it appears at your side. It bears something in its closed hand. It opens its fingers, and in its palm you see a perfect jewel. Its hue is the colour you most need to absorb from your angel, and from the angelic worlds, for your healing and spiritual liberation. Place the jewel within your heart-centre, and see the mystery and sweetness of the spiritual colour as it flashes and scintillates within your heart, sending the bright song of its colour throughout every level on which you resonate.

Air

Focus on the quiet in-breath and out-breath of the rhythm of your breathing. You open your inner eyes to find yourself in an orchard. The first spring-green leaves are upon the fruit trees, and in the wide grassy spaces between the tree boles are carpets of honey-scented blue-bells, dancing in the light breeze. Your guardian angel appears before you in the spring sunshine. It extends great golden, encircling wings that vibrate and beat in coruscations of light. Placing its hand lightly on your shoulder, your guardian angel encourages you to unfurl your own wings. Beautiful white wings composed of pulsating waves of radiance begin to unfold from your spine, so that they stretch from above your head to your feet.

Beating your wings in time with your angel, you rise into the air until you are far above the treetops. In the perfect blue of a springtime sky, you dive and loop and sky-dance with your angel in a joyful celebration of freedom, vivification and weightlessness. Light as thistledown, you soar into the heart of the sweet sparkling blue, and rest on the gentle air currents like a feather on the breath of God. Surrender to deep, deep stillness, deep, deep rest.

At your side as you lie in your cradle of air, your guardian angel evokes a perfume from its heart-centre that fills all your being with the peace and delight of its fragrance. Its hallowed scent is that which opens your inner senses so that you are transported into the wonder of the spiritual worlds.

The four elements can be considered as the four wondrous rivers that run through paradise (spoken of in many esoteric and religious texts, and particularly in Islam). They are a manifestation of the mystery of the Godhead. As their vibrational essence is reduced to the level of physical expression so that they may flow into and create our world, they become the four marvels of earth, water, air and fire, which are subject to pollution and corruption due to the nature of matter. The elements are within *us*, they comprise our physical bodies, and their refined essence expresses itself through our thoughts and feelings. Until we learn to rule them by the authority of the spiritual light whose flame is in our heart-centre, they maintain an elemental overlordship and oppress the freedom of the soul. We suffer from wrath (the rage of fire), depression and perceptual blindness (the darkness of earth), the destruction of rampant desires and emotionalism (the inundation of water) and the distortion, imbalance and arrogance of the mental faculties when they have become separated from the wisdom of the soul and the light of the spirit (the power of winds that blow us off course, and the chaos inherent in philosophies ruled by 'hot air').

The elements are our great teachers. We have to make an effort each day, virtually with each breath, to overcome their elemental rule and achieve self-mastery.

Thus do we overcome all the oppressions of the soul, and throw off the chains of our attachment to matter and the consciousness of matter in its corrupt state, which is materialism. Our guardian angel is appointed to us to help with this great and arduous, but joyful, task of liberation.

When we perceive the truth of the nature of the elements, we see that the earth is an expression of jewels and treasures of discovery, wondrous to behold and beautiful beyond imagining; that water is the very essence of the ethereal loveliness of the soul; that the winds are the impassioned movement of Almighty Spirit, its flight and its fragrant breath; and that fire is the creative principle itself, an inconceivable, ineffable and eternal flame.

The Secret of The Star

The six-pointed star is used in each of these visualizations. It is a powerful symbol, integrating our earthly yet spiritually aspiring selves (represented by the upward-pointing pyramid or equilateral triangle) with our higher self or spirit that dwells within the realm of the Divine (the downward-pointing pyramid or equilateral triangle). When the two fuse and become one, the 'mystical marriage' between soul and spirit is achieved, and a star is created which blazes forth with a surpassingly beautiful radiance. (In *The Secret Teachings of Mary Magdalene* which I have written with my friend, Margaret Bailey, we explain how this magical fusion point is the 'nous', of which Christ said in the Gospel of Mary Magdalene – 'Where the nous is, there lies the treasure.' When we create the star, the 'nous' is activated, and we *become* the star.)

This symbol of the six-pointed star, which is like the Star of David except that it has no inner divisions, is the most powerful image we can use to gain access to our higher self and to the angelic worlds. Its dynamic force cannot be harnessed for anything other than positive, beautiful, spiritual purposes, and we find it and ignite it by gently focusing on our heart-centre and the rhythm of our breathing. We see the star with the eye of the imagination, but its marvellous healing influence, inspiration and blessing is an alchemy that we directly experience.

The imagination, consciously wielded in its higher aspect from the heart, is a power far more meaningful and mightier in its scope and magnitude than we have been permitted to realize. It is, indeed, the God-power, given to us as an immeasurably precious gift by the Godhead when in its boundless grace it made us in its own 'image'. So, with your imagination, make the star; use it and dwell in it. It is the source of the true life deep within your soul, your veritable spirit, and it will release you from illusion and suffering.

We can also use this sacred star to bless others – our animal and human friends, our environment, Mother Earth herself – and it is indeed part of our guardian angel's work to inspire us to do so. Just see the six-pointed star in your heart-centre, blazing with a pure and infinitely bright light – the light of heaven – and, using the gentle rhythm of your breath, breathe out its light to our suffering world. The angels and the creative forces have their own beautiful rhythm, and when we attune ourselves to this holy breath, we work hand in hand with angels.

The Angelic Hours

An angel is appointed guardianship over every hour of the day and night, as many legends, biblical stories and fairy tales attest (consider the story of the 12 dancing princesses). The angelic rhythm referred to, however, which is also our own spiritual rhythm, follows the pattern of 3, 6, 9 and 12 as these hours are counted by the hands on the clock face throughout each cycle of 24. The rhythm is not affected by seasonal adjustments.

Twelve noon, the heart-centre of each day, is the most powerful of all the rhythmic hours; but creating the star and sending out its light on the cusp of any of the magical hours of 3, 6, 9 and 12 (or indeed any hour or any time), is always of the utmost benefit, and will assuredly help to lift the Earth and her humanity into the healing, wisdom and renewal which are contained within the light of the spirit. Nevertheless, attuning to the rhythm of the magical hours of 3, 6, 9 and 12 gives an added impetus and power to our spiritual work and unfoldment.

There are three aspects to the visualization of the star in the heart. We find it deep within, secreted in our innermost, in our heart of hearts. At the same time, we truly have our existence in the heart of the star itself; and so, when we attune ourselves to the star, we also need to think of ourselves as secure in its centre. Simultaneously, we see the star shining above our heads; not far away in the sky but no further than the distance of a treetop – just enough to remind us that the star is our inspiration and our aspiration.

Giving Gifts to Our Angels

The following is a prayer for humanity that we can offer as a gift to our guardian angel, and to the group of angels with which it works, in return for all the loving service they give to us in every area of our lives. Despite this tender and meticulous attention to the smallest detail of our needs, our angels constantly balance the nurture of the microcosm with the ultimate realization and destination of the macrocosm. It is their dearest wish that we, in our turn, never lose sight of the bigger picture, and are never petty or isolationist in our aims or our philosophy.

It is the mission of the Brotherhood of Angels and Humanity to bring about a state of life on earth which will enable every member of creation to wholly unfold their spiritual gifts and potential so that each dwells in happiness and harmony, one with another, liberated from suffering and limitation. This state is not so far off as we might think! Nor, are we assured, is it any impossibly romantic ideal. The angels have given us this maxim: 'Nothing is too beautiful to be true.'

The guardian angel will bring to us numerous opportunities to serve the angels in our daily lives – little openings for a kind and cheering word, a gesture of non-judgemental support, an encouraging smile, the chance to give comfort and hope and reassurance. These little services can make a vast difference to people's lives and can be a veritable lifeline for some. As we take up these opportunities, so more will come.

We have to be careful of our lower mind, the mind of earth, which wants to disinherit us from the attainment of our true destiny, and will tell us to leave it, move on, not to get involved, we will probably only embarrass ourselves or make things worse, we haven't got the time, it's none of our business anyway. Take no notice of this little wretch, and refuse to let it be your master! It operates by making us panic when we go against its dreary dictates; but don't worry, the panic is soon overcome and you will feel a new, liberating power stirring within you – a truly angelic power.

Remember, also, that the angels will always safeguard us from unwarranted intrusion in our lives if we will listen to their wisdom. Doing the angels' work on earth is not a question of calling difficult people and situations to us so that our path becomes blocked. The angels will teach us to help others without becoming entangled.

One sure way in which we can serve the angels every day is by taking the time (just a few minutes) to give forth the Prayer for Humanity at noon, or one of the other angelic hours (3,6,9,12). Every time we do this, we help to change the world.

Prayer for Humanity

Go to the heart-centre and peacefully watch the light shining there in the form of a perfect, six-pointed star (without inner divisions such as the Star of David bears).

Gently breathe in the light until it fills all your being, and see the star appear as a huge radiant form above you. Feel simultaneously that you are in the heart of the star, that it is above you, and also shining in your own heart. All of this should take only a few seconds.

Now say, aloud or silently:

'We hold all humankind in the golden light of the heavenly star, and see the power of the Divine Child* working in the heart of every member of humanity.

'We behold the blazing star, with the form of the Son-Daughter of Light within its centre, radiating the spirit of divine love, peace and healing power over all the earth, to all humanity.

'We see the earthly brethren of all races and all faiths together in brotherhood, at one in the Star of Illumination and Peace.

'We hold all those who have asked for help and healing in the radiance of this great healing star. (Name anyone known to you personally who is in need or who has asked for help.)

*See Appendix I.

'May the magic of the star shining from our hearts bring healing to our animal brethren, to all the world of nature and her spirits, and to our beloved Mother Earth.

'May the blessing of God-Goddess be on this work.

'Amen.'

Further Gifts to the Angels

At times during each day, whenever you think of it, go to your heart-centre and say silently or aloud, 'Angels, speed on wings of light and healing to wherever you are needed in the world.' Angels need this invitation from humans in order to be able to work to their full capacity for our good.

Take 30-second breaks throughout the day, tuning in through the heart-centre to an ascending dove of peace, a serene yellow lotus-flower (like a water lily) or a perfect rose, the colour of a flush-pink sunrise. Just hold the image peacefully for half a minute, as if you were looking into a different, radiant world, entirely filled with this single mysterious image.

The angels will use these moments as opportunities to instruct, enlighten, heal and guide you, not always through messages but through a quality of love or happiness that steals gently into the heart like a ray of sunshine.

It is worth remembering that one enlightened soul or 'starseed' can raise the vibrations of 10,000 blinkered souls, so that they too become bathed in light. Our angels are all around us, our guardian angel and our own angel group, always ready to link us to any angel whose services we might need, from the highest to the humblest. Stay in touch with your angels and make full use of the magical star within your heart-centre. That seed of light is the indwelling miracle which will transform ourselves and our world.

⟁ A N G E L I C   S E E D - T H O U G H T S   ⟁

You will find these scattered throughout this book. They are
thoughts, given to us by spiritual masters, poets, philosophers,
dreamers and seers. which were implanted and fostered by angels,
and which bear an angelic essence. Use them by dwelling tranquilly
on the words and allowing your mind to be softly absorbed into your
heart-centre. Therein, the angels will impart to you the full shining
significance of their vision, so that the words spring to life and take
flight as birds of the soul. Here is the first scattering:

> *Every rose that is sweet-scented is telling of the*
> *secrets of the Universal.*

> **Rumi (from Masnavi 1:2022)**

> *There is only one moment in time when it is*
> *essential to awaken.*
> *That moment is now.*

> **Buddha**

> *The Valley Spirit never dies.*
> *It is called the Mysterious Female.*
> *And the doorway of the Mysterious Female*
> *is the base from which Heaven and Earth spring.*
> *It is there within us all the time. Draw upon it as*
> *you will, it never runs dry.*

> **Lao Tzu**

No man shall ever know what is true blessedness
Till oneness overwhelm and swallow separateness.

Angelus Silesius

ANGEL CONTEMPLATION

We urge you to give a thought to
angel messengers each day of your lives,
for they will bless you
with the joy and the beauty
of the spiritual worlds.

For a brief time, in the silence of spirit,
listen.
Listen to their message.
It may be soundless and wordless –
but in your heart will come a stillness
and a love not usually known
on the outer planes.

And from this spiritual river
flowing to you at flood tide from the angels
you can draw water for others
to drink and bathe in
according to their need.

White Eagle

CHAPTER TWO

COMMUNING WITH OUR GUARDIAN ANGEL

Part One

In the following two chapters, we will discuss methods of connecting and communing with our guardian angel. There are many ways to open the channel between our guardian angel and ourselves, and it is certainly not necessary to diligently pursue every single one explained below in order to establish contact. Nevertheless, several of the methods and foci described are indispensable, in particular; imagination, breath, the heart-centre, the chakras, stilling the mind and the emotions, meditation, heart-to-heart communion and grounding. These are the secrets upon which communion with our guardian angel is founded.

Finding the Name of Our Angel

Some people feel much more comfortable if they know their guardian angel's name as they begin to develop their skills of angelic communion. I have never felt the need to know the name of my angel, perhaps because I like the sound of the term 'guardian angel' – but it is a rather long-winded title if you need to call on your angel in a crisis!

Here is a method we can use to discover the name of our guardian angel:

Sit in meditation, using the Rose Mandala as your focus.

The patterns are initiatory and mystical dancing paths to the Sacred Centre. Gently become aware of them.

Let yourself be absorbed into them, and let your soul dance within them. When you are ready, ask aloud for the name of your guardian angel.

Repeat the process and ask for the collective name of your group of angels.

(This may be strange — mine are called 'the Hill of Flame'!) The answer will be spoken clearly into your mind's ear.

You can find out the name of any of your individual angels by applying this method.

You may want to know the name of your business angel, your angel of the home, your garden angel, your writing/painting/composing angel, your inspirational angel, your interior-decorating angel, your computer angel, and so on. Whatever activity you are involved in, if it is creative and task-based, an angel is designated to help you with it. Your guardian angel will connect you to these angels, fostering and ministering to the working relationship with which you enter into with them.

Writing to Our Guardian Angel

This method is a very simple and direct method of communing with our guardian angel. Take the time to use it almost every day, if you can, and you will be intrigued with the results!

Use white paper (preferably unlined) or coloured paper that corresponds to the colour (or one of the colours) of your angel. (See pages 35–6)

Ground yourself (imagine strong, rope-like roots growing from the soles of your feet down into the centre of the

earth and anchoring themselves firmly there – the process need only take a few seconds).

In your imagination, light a candle in honour of the guardian angel before you begin writing. When you have a very important question to put to your angel, you might like to light a real candle. Again, let it be white, or of a colour emanated by your angel.

Don't meditate. Just relax.

Go to the heart-centre.

Breathe in the light which shines there and breathe it out, in gentle rhythm.

Ask your question, or communicate anything on your mind to your angel, by writing it down.

The angel's response will come through you. Sometimes, when I explain this exercise, people don't realize that I mean it quite literally. Via your agency, the angel will write back to you. Don't think or concentrate in a tense way. Be at ease and let the angelic communication stream through you in written words. The sensation will be as if you are listening intently and taking everything down, like a secretary. Often the answers come so fast, it is difficult to keep up!

Close by thanking your angel. Keep its messages for future reference, because you will be amazed to see how accurate and meaningful its responses are, sometimes all the more so after the passage of a little time.

Take care to connect properly with the heart chakra. If you connect with the solar plexus, your desire body will take over and you will write what you want to hear! If you only connect with the head-centres, you will write what you think you ought to hear! In neither case will it be true angelic communication. The other chakras are used by the angels to communicate with us, but the initial contact must be made via the point of stillness and balance in the heart.

Basics of Angel Communication

Imagination — The Divine Faculty Connecting Us to Truth

When we were given the revelation that we are made in God's image, it intimated – not that God-Goddess looks like the average man or woman walking down the street – but that we were given the creative power of the Godhead as a special grace. It dwells within us. That creative principle is the imagination. Everything that comes into being has to be *imagined* first, even the simplest, humblest things. Learn to trust and to revere your imagination. It is the golden key to the spiritual worlds.

Imagination is our divine gift – a window on truth – a tool for inner sight. When the imagination and the intuition work hand in hand, you will truly be able to walk with angels. They are almost the same faculty. Imagination is the clarity of seeing, intuition is the wisdom of knowing. Samandriel is the angel who presides over and blesses the imagination. Brigid is the goddess who succours the imagination and the intuition, in her role as mistress of creative fire and the crystal clarity of the soul. Always there are the two aspects feeding us in life – the angelic life-stream on the one hand, and the human on the other.

If you have difficulty in using your imagination, or faculty of creative visualization, begin by endeavouring to see in your mind's eye some simple objects, such as different fruits. Imagine a bright yellow banana, a shiny red apple, a golden pear, a round, smooth hazelnut. Picture them one by one as vividly as you can, and hold them in mental focus for as long as is comfortable. Then repeat the exercise; only this time, as you create them in your imagination, also imagine their taste. Make them delicious – the very best banana, apple, pear and hazel nut, etc., that you have ever tasted. Soon, your imagination, with all its subtle inner senses, will begin to awaken within you, and you will be thrilled by the new worlds that will begin to open up to you.

Once you have accomplished a clear visualization of the fruits, you may like to progress to the meditations given below. The first is a simple, short introduction to Samandriel, so that you might be led to a revelation of her mysteries. The second meditation is more complex. It involves the presence of a unicorn, the creature of enchantment 'that never was'. The unicorn does exist, but we must open the door onto its realms with the key of the imagination. The unicorn is a symbol of the soul, and of the gifts of imagination and intuition that are its treasures. Its horn signifies the higher, exalted intelligence that is bestowed on us through the activation of soul vision, which is fed by the principles of the imaginative and intuitive faculties.

If you experience difficulty in using your imagination and its essential component – visualization – practise with the visualization exercise and the shorter meditation first before progressing to 'The Candle of Vision'. The latter can be tape-recorded so that it may serve as a traditional creative visualization exercise, or, alternatively, it can simply be read in a relaxed frame of mind, taking time to inwardly experience each stage of the journey it offers, so that it becomes a 'reading meditation' (a light meditation that does not take you too far within, but does offer the absorbing spell of sacred storytelling, thus giving the perceptual apparatus we use in more advanced meditation a thorough 'workout').

The Blessing of Samandriel

Focus gently on your breathing, and listen to the sound of its rhythm, until you feel yourself entering the silence within.

You are sitting before a bright mirror, lit with the soft effulgence of the full moon, which shines above you. Look into the depths of the mirror.

An angel appears in the mirror. Contemplate her beauty and perfection, her spiritual mystery. She is the Angel Samandriel, offering you three gifts. The first is purity; the second is abundance; the third is guided and

protected entry into the mirror, which is your imagination. This third gift is a crystal key.

Graciously accept her gifts; return her loving smile, and
step into the mirror with Samandriel, your guide. Dwell
there with her awhile, receiving as further gifts the revelations she gives to you, until you are ready to return to
normal consciousness.

The Candle of Vision

Sit in a comfortable and relaxed position, spine straight,
supported if necessary, focus your awareness at your
heart-centre and softly draw the breath 'through the
heart', breathing a little more slowly and deeply than
usual.

Light a white candle or create a lucid image of a lighted
candle.

With gentle concentration, sit and watch your candle for a
while. It is the Candle of Vision, and in your higher
awareness you know that its unearthly counterpart burns
brightly and unquenchably. You know, too, that it is as if
the candle with its glowing flame were truly a mirror, for
in your heart-centre your eternal self coruscates like a
spearhead of light and can never be extinguished.

Focus now on that flame in your heart, ever giving forth a
soft, holy radiance which would light up all your being
and all your life if you would allow it to do so. It is the
light of peace, emanating from a great cosmic heart of
love.

Keep that still flame in your mind's eye as you go deeper
into the inner worlds, even though other visions rise and
unfold before you.

You are standing at the margin of a mountainside
woodland. Little mists white as virgin snow curl and weave
upon its floor, and bracing and vigorous airs blow about it
and make the trees rustle softly and strangely, with an
almost articulate voice. It is sunrise, early in the spring,

and the morning wears the garments of winter but dances with the spirit of summer in all her delight and promise.

The mountain breeze is so clean and cool and life-giving that you feel that you are at the very edge of the world, watching the first dawn break. The colours in the sky are a great spreading mystery of crimson, brilliant as the flashing of a jewel, of drifting rose, sweet gold and muted celandine, sparkling white-silver and soft angel blue. There is magic in this sunrise, and as if to verify your recognition of it, a voice calls your name from the depths of the sunny wood.

You hardly know if the voice is real or imaginary, but you are moved to respond to it anyway by a deep soul impulse. You walk into the flowering woods.

As sweet aromas arise from the bracken and the fresh, wholesome earth, you become aware of other perfumes, flower scents and the delicate incense of the first blue-bells of the year, creating enchanted pools below the trees. They give forth a wild fragrance, as of the essence of carefree childhood happiness, and from their midst a bird of beautiful song flies up and perches on a branch just above your head, pouring out its rapture to the morning in a mellifluent flood of bell-like, crystal notes.

It is a woodlark, and as you engage with his bright eye you realize that he is leading you to some secret, lovely place, deep in the magical woodland.

As you pass a huge, majestic oak wound around with ivy, you enter a wide glade that, breathtakingly, is a sequestered garden set like a mystic jewel in the heart of the wood.

Birds of many colours flit from branch to branch, and everywhere you look, full of wonder, burgeoning flowers of every dream-engendered hue climb and twine and pour from bushes or glow among the grass like a meeting of rivers from the heart of paradise.

Entranced, you gaze around at the radiant inner forms of

the trees and the flowers, at the soft emerald grass at your feet, at the rainbow wealth of the flowers.

You inhale their perfume and consider their perfection of form. Every leaf, every blade, every petal shares the sublime consciousness of the Great Spirit, of the dancing Goddess. And now you, the pilgrim soul, are looking into the mystical heart of the garden with eyes of the spirit.

Where is this mystical heart of the garden?

You know where it lies because the point of consciousness where it dwells is given to you, as if by the whisper of the Goddess, as if on the breath of angels.

Look deep, deep into this mystical heart and begin to see a soul-form taking shape... that of the bright-white, lightly tripping unicorn, mighty and ancient of spirit, kindly and gentle of demeanour, of grace and beauty measureless, radiating a hallowed peace.

Your deeper self is about to receive the shining vision of the unicorn into its heart.

You see its horn, gleaming golden-white, its white flanks shining with a pure radiance, its fathomless eyes alight with a strange glory which pierces your heart with a shaft of divine love.

The unicorn recognizes you, knows you! It was the voice of the unicorn which called to you so that you responded to its bidding and came in search of the miracle of its being.

Bathe in the wonder and the gladness and the deep heart-peace of this moment, and in your turn begin to call out to the unicorn.

Let it be a call from your soul to your spirit. You do not need to use words; just allow this soul-call to rise up and to go forth from your heart.

Alerted, the unicorn raises its noble head. Its rippling white mane moves in the winds of the spirit. Responding, its body poised in heavenly radiance, it takes its first steps towards you.

Hold out your arms to embrace it as it walks to where you are waiting.

Let your meeting be a delight and an awakening.

It will allow you to mount its back, for you and this magical being are destined to take many spiritual journeys together, adventuring deep into the heaven worlds.

The unicorn carries you to a place in the wood where you begin to climb upwards. Soon the trees fall away and you are tripping across wild open moorland. Always you are aware of the unicorn's golden-white horn, going before you like the still, golden-white flame in your heart.

You pass pools surrounded by knotgrass on your upward climb that shake with a strange dark light in which are reflected your own shining soul alight with its flame of spirit, the shining white unicorn who carries you and the many faces of the One Great Goddess, who sometimes appears as remote and austere and more often as loving and reassuring. Ravens, curlews, wild geese and lapwings circle and call into the wind.

You and your unicorn come upon an ancient grave, a small barrow mound set in the midst of a stone circle, wild and lonely.

The unicorn carries you within.

The grave is the mouth to the underworld.

Together you penetrate the still, deep fastnesses of the underworld, and you begin to realize in wonder that your underworld journey is leading you to the Heart of the Holy Mountain, wherein burns the Sacred and Eternal Flame.

All the protectors of the inner sanctum of the Holy Mountain allow the unicorn to proceed, for it stands surety for your soul. You come to the chamber where the Holy Flame eternally burns, enshrined in an altar formed from the living rock.

Four great guardians stand around it, nature beings which are part god and part angel.

You kneel, with your unicorn before you, at the foot of the altar. You see your unicorn take a single gazelle-like spring, and enter the Sacred and Eternal Flame. The horn of the unicorn and the tall, majestic flame become one.

The guardians instruct you and offer their blessings, each in their turn.

First, the Guardian of the North steps forward. Listen to his words, receive his blessing.

Then the Guardian of the South steps forward. Listen to her words, receive her blessing.

Now the Guardian of the East steps forward. Listen to his words, receive his blessing.

Lastly, the Guardian of the West steps forward. Listen to her words, receive her blessing.

The guardians silently withdraw, and leave you in adoration of the Sacred and Eternal Flame.

The Holy Flame silently scintillates until the flame in your own heart rises and leaps, and you and the Sacred and Eternal Flame are one, linked by your heart.

Gradually, the silent flame becomes a blazing star, a perfect Star of Peace, which irradiates every part of the chamber, every part of your being, and shines out with powerful radiance into the world.

You see that every member of humanity, every sentient being on all planes of existence, bathes in the heart-light given out by the flame and enters into a state of peace.

You feel yourself being gently drawn upwards, rising through the air in soul-flight. You pass through the solid rock of the mountain as if it were no more than transparent mist, safe in a channel of spiritual light.

The great sky breaks upon your vision, clear and mystic blue. You are upon the Holy Mountaintop, and above you the immeasurable Star gives forth its flood of ineffable love, ineffable power, ineffable peace over all the earth, silently, magically, eternally.

You know that it shines through you, through your heart-centre; and that to heal yourself and to heal the world, you have only to link with it consciously and give it forth.

Place the symbol of the bright silver cross in a circle of white light upon your crown, brow, throat, heart and solar plexus.

Go on your way, enlightened by the knowledge that your unicorn will always walk with you, there to respond to your call when you next wish to meet with it in the exquisite garden at the heart of the magical wood, bringing with it joy, delight, guiding wisdom and the balm of peace unbounded from the spiritual worlds, where the Star is eternally shining.

Breath

We communicate with our guardian angel via our breath – through air. We need to breathe gently and a little more deeply than usual when preparing to commune with our angel. Our guardian angel connects us to other angels whose assistance we need, and helps to shine their qualities into our soul through the magical power of our breath. Angels enter into us through the symbol of air, the supreme symbol of brotherhood; for we all breathe the same air. Do angels breathe? They do; but their respiration draws on the refined spiritual essence of the element of air – what air is, we might say, before it is lowered in vibration and becomes mundane, physical and corruptible.

It is of benefit to take the time to be still and to dwell on our breathing as a sacred act. Mary Magdalene's gospel tells us, 'Those that listen will hear the breath of Silence.' When we practise sacred breathing, we listen to the rhythm of our breath; this draws us gently into the Silence, that point of peace within the heart which is the threshold of the spiritual worlds.

A beautiful and ancient Sanskrit mantra is 'Ham Sah'. This intonation imitates the sound of the in-breath and the out-breath.

'Ham' is spoken as you breathe in, and comprises the affirmation 'I
Am'. 'Sah' is spoken as you breathe out, and means the sacred flame
in the heart, the 'nous', the Divine Spark – our spiritual reality
which is our true self.

The wonderful healing art of the guardian angel is evident in a
simple breathing exercise.

As you breathe in, collect together all your fears, frets,
hastes and anxieties.

Hold the breath a moment, and see these swirling nega-
tivities contained in a transparent blue balloon.

Breathe out all your worries. as if you are emptying the
balloon, into the arms of your angel. He or she will take
them all from you, and gently bear them away.

Breathe in again, and this time, see the blue balloon fill
with sunshine and happiness.

Breathe out, and feel the peace of the joyful sunshine
wash over you.

—◦ ANGELIC SEED-THOUGHTS ◦—

Where the nous is,
there lies the treasure.
When you find the treasure,
therein lies the breath of infinite vision.

Mary Magdalene
(from *The Secret Teachings of Mary Magdalene*, by
Claire Nahmad and Margaret Bailey)

Breathing in I calm body and mind,
Breathing out I smile.
Dwelling in the present moment,
I know this is the only moment.

Thich Nhat Hanh
(from *The Miracle of Mindfulness*)

The Heart-Centre

Although our guardian angel also makes use of our other chakras in its communion with us (chakras are points of power within our physical body that connect us to the inner worlds of the Divine) we always communicate with our guardian, and with the group of angels that tend us, via the heart-centre. This is our innermost shrine, our holiest altar. It is our *nous*, the point where the soul and spirit meet and become one.

Because the breath and the heart are such essential components of angelic communication, we have to combine the two. We do this by 'breathing through the heart'. Just imagine that you are drawing each incoming breath in through the heart, and releasing each outgoing breath out through the heart. It is a simple and natural process; and, somehow, the act of breathing itself seems easier, and to extend in capacity, when we thus 'breathe through the heart'.

An effective method of practising the art of 'breathing through the heart' is followed by linking our imagination to the symbol of the Sacred and Eternal Flame as we do the breathing exercise. The meditation below can be used to achieve this. Practise 'breathing through the heart' as you progress through the meditation or guided visualization (it will become a meditation if you enter very deeply into the experience, or remain a guided visualization if you simply read the words and follow the imagery in a contemplative or light meditative state). When you come to the healing chant ('The Secret of the Flame'), let the words flow through your mind in chanting waves of sound. Summon them in silence, listen to them,

and keep breathing through your heart-centre. You will find that
the rhythm of the chant becomes the rhythm of your breathing.

The Sacred and Eternal Flame

Sit comfortably, spine upright, supported if necessary,
and breathe quietly and easily through the heart-centre.

For this meditation you are asked to prepare yourself for
a spiritual journey to Tibet.

You will project yourself by means of your creative imagination deep into the Himalayas, and penetrate the secret
recesses of a holy mountain in order to learn from
Buddhist wisdom the simple and beautiful mystery of life
itself, in which lies the secret of enduring peace. You will
experience it as a melding into one of your heart-centre,
your breathing, and the perfect, still radiance of the
Sacred and Eternal Flame.

Begin to imagine that you are in a great monastery,
ancient and sacred, deeply sequestered within the hollow
of a mountain.

You are being led by one of the elder brethren to a most
holy place. Feel the worn smoothness of the stone corri-
dors beneath your feet, and the rougher ridges of the walls
as your robes brush against them. Hear the faint echoes of
bells and distant chanting – a reassuring, soothing sound.

Your guide leads you to a chamber wherein stands a
simple altar. The altar is fashioned from the living rock
and enshrines a single flame – the Sacred and Eternal
Flame which is the mystery of all life, all creation.

You are ushered into the presence of the Sacred and
Eternal Flame.

You are led to a place in front of the altar. You sit comfortably, and in peace and reverence you meditate upon
the flame. Your guide withdraws silently, but you can feel
her or his protective presence nearby.

The flame burns steadily, steadily, never flickering, never

growing less. The flame is still, perfect in shape like two hands held, peaceful and poised, in prayer. Its colour is white, shining white, alive with a wonderful vibrancy which is happiness, which is peace, which is blessedness.

Now the Sacred and Eternal Flame reveals its deepest secret to you.

Your vision is withdrawn into your inner self. You see your own heart like a little cave. Within the cave burns the pure white light, the Sacred and Eternal Flame which is the source of your being. You know that in the heart of every man, woman and child, there burns this perfect light, the Sacred and Eternal Flame of the Heart.

Now contemplate in silence the words of the healing chant, the Secret of the Flame:

'I meditate deeply upon the Sacred and Eternal Flame which burns in my heart. I know that it is the pure essence of all life, all being, all creation. I know that it burns in the heart of every man, every woman, every child. Within the heart of all creation burns the Sacred and Eternal Flame, the shining white light.

'I now affirm everlasting brotherhood with all people, with all sentient beings, with all life, with our beautiful planet Mother Earth. The Sacred and Eternal Flame is the essence of divine and universal love and it has the power to overcome every problem of my mind, my heart, my soul and my life.

'The white light of Love is healing and restoring and beautifying every atom of my mind, my body, my consciousness. I am in the light and the light is all.'

Now let the flame in your heart flower into the perfect shape of a six-pointed star which shines eternally above you in the spiritual skies. These are the celestial realms, not the sky of earth but of the everlasting worlds within our own consciousness, the key to which dwells in the heart, where the Sacred and Eternal Flame is to be found.

Meditate upon the shining six-pointed star.

When you are ready, descend to earth again, safe in your ring of light. Seal your chakras with the bright silver star encircled by a ring of light, and affirm:

I am enfolded within the heart of peace;

I am enfolded within the heart of love;

I am in the light and the light is all.

Gently bring your meditation to a close.

—◦ ANGELIC SEED-THOUGHTS ◦—

Attune to the heart through the breath.
Be at one with oneself and the universe;
and your body (matter) will become blessed
as nothingness (no longer a 'thing'),
a pulsating life-force
resonant with the message of Breath.

Mary Magdalene (from *The Secret Teachings of Mary Magdalene* by Claire Nahmad and Margaret Bailey)

The great wind of life (Breath)
scatters us to the four corners.
This is the structure that will teach us
how to return to the centre.
When we are born as an out-breath
of the Great Spirit,
all our desire must be
to find the in-breath in ourselves
which will carry us back home.
When we find it,

the in-breath and the out-breath
become as one.

Both proceed from the heart of giving
which is the centre,
and the centre is everywhere,
even where the great wind of life scatters us
to the four corners.

Mary Magdalene (from *The Secret Teachings of Mary*
***Magdalene* by Claire Nahmad and Margaret Bailey)**

The Chakras

Our seven main chakras are the base chakra, at the base of the spine; our sacral chakra, just below the naval; our solar plexus chakra; our heart chakra; our throat chakra, in the hollow of the throat; our brow chakra, on the ridge of our brow, between the eyes; and our double crown chakra, one of which corresponds with our crown and is seated in the middle of the brain, the other being situated at the top of the forehead, in the centre. Although our guardian angel will use other chakras to communicate with us, especially the throat chakra, initial contact is always made via the heart. (The chakras will be dealt with more fully in a later chapter.)

To draw closer to your guardian angel, and to discover which of your chakras it prefers to use in its communion with you, you can use a short and simple dedication ceremony which I have set out below. The ceremony will lead you to discover, not only the main chakra or chakras through which it prefers to communicate with you, but also the colour or colours with which your angel resonates.

To help this process (it is not always necessary), you might like to hold a sheet of pure white paper in your hands as you perform the ceremony. When you ask your guardian angel to give you its colour, gently gaze at the centre of the paper. Don't stare or strain your eyes; just let your vision softly rest on the paper. The colour of the angel will be subtly reflected onto its surface. You may, of course, prefer not to use the paper, and to use your inner sight only. Because this is a ceremony dedicated to your guardian angel, light a white candle in honour of your angel, if possible, before you begin.

Dedication Ceremony to Your Guardian Angel

Be still, and open your heart to the Divine Presence.

Within your heart is a perfect six-pointed star, shining with a holy light.

Look deep into the centre of this peacefully shining star.

See, in the heart of the star, a radiant angel form with wings of light outstretched, indescribably brilliant, so calm and still, remote from the material plane, yet all love.

Say in your heart, 'I request and accept the love, the guidance and the service of my guardian angel, and of all my angel friends.'

The Angel of the Star greets you with a glad welcome and enfolds you in its great wings. From its shining heart, your guardian angel takes flight towards you.

You are accepted into the Brotherhood of Angels and Humanity.

Three gifts are given to you by the angel.

They are: a colour... accept it, remember it;

a light touch on one of your chakras; remember which one;

an image or a sign... what is it?

The guardian angel speaks: 'Wherever you walk, you will be enfolded in my wings and accompanied by angels. Be at peace. All is well. Amen.'

Close the ceremony by blowing out the candle, aware as you do so that your breath is holy and can give forth blessings, and send your love and thanks to your angel.

—๑   A N G E L I C   S E E D - T H O U G H T S   ๑—

Open your heart, and let the heart-centre
open the chakras.
Within the heart is the nous.
Through the nous, listen to the Breath.
The Breath of life is All.

**Mary Magdalene (from *The Secret Teachings of Mary
Magdalene* by Claire Nahmad and Margaret Bailey)**

Where the star shines by the will and
through the love of earthly men and women,
the effect over chaos and disorder, war,
and all the evils in the world, can be truly
magical.

White Eagle (from *The Book of Star Light*)

Still the Mind and the Emotions

Tranquillity, and a disciplined mental and emotional body, will lead
us into deep and true communion with our guardian angel. This
does not mean that we cannot turn to our angel when all kinds of
turbulent emotions are rushing through us; such straitened times
are exactly when we should call on our angel for help; nevertheless,
we cannot enter into deep communion, transmitting and receiving
at a profound inner level so that we are actually in heart-to-heart
discourse with our angel, until we find the point of peace within.
This is achieved by focusing on our breath and going to our heart-
centre – letting the mind softly sink into the heart – as has
previously been discussed.

The soothing contemplation on that point of peace that follows will help to lead you to that magical place in the heart where peace dwells:

PEACE IS WITHIN

Find the point of peace within.

It dwells not in the mind,

Not in the turbulent emotional body,

But deep in the heart, like a tranquil jewel.

Give up the haughty claims of the mind,

Give up the anxiety-spell of the emotional body;

Go straight to the heart.

Like a babe enfolded in the embrace of its mother,

Peace will hold you in everlasting arms;

It is a rose softly lit with the light of eternity.

Within its temple you receive true Selfhood.

Your in-breath partakes of its holy essence.

You breathe out its fragrance to heal the world.

Trust

We need to trust. A guardian angel gave us this message concerning trust:

Trust is the soil

which will grow the garden

wherein you and your angel may walk.

Trust the angels; trust what comes to you, trust the guidance flowing to you from your guardian angel.

Two Points

- The angels never demand from or dictate to us.
- They respect our free will.

Their guidance is wise and gentle. If they want to encourage us to make a big leap of faith, to change something fundamental in our lives, they suggest a series of steps towards it. They don't overturn our lives in a dramatic way; they never force decisions on us. Sometimes they do want us to take a chance on something, but they will guide us through the steps to our decision very lovingly and gently, like supportive friends with only our good at heart, which of course is exactly what they are.

Meditation and the Mystery of the Soul

Meditation is essential to the unfolding of our awareness of our guardian angel, and of the inner worlds of spiritual beauty that it inhabits. Without meditation, we will find that we can only progress so far in our relationship and communion with our guardian angel and the angelic brethren with which it seeks to link us. The great task and purpose of our angel is to awaken our soul, the 'wedding garment', so that the soul embraces and resonates with the spiritual spark that resides within us all, that spark which is our true individuality, and which is a mystic flame of Divine Spirit. Every other aspect of us, from the subtlest down to the coarsest outer layer (which is our physical being), is actually only a body. Even our soul is only a body; but it is a body of such exquisite sensitivity, beauty and hallowed mystery that it bears the potential within it to receive the baptism of eternal life that can only be vouchsafed by Divine Spirit. Once this has occurred, the soul and the spirit become one being, an individuated being divine and eternal and ready to co-create with God.

It came as an unpleasant shock to me to realize that we are actually capable of destroying our souls. Spiritual masters, and the angels themselves, teach that this is so; and yet, when we consider how we set about systematically destroying our own bodies, and even that sacred encompassing body, the planet Earth herself, we might more easily comprehend this disturbing concept. Of course, the life of the Godhead in all its expressions is the supreme principle of existence, and its unassailable law. Such life can never be destroyed, because death has no dominion over it.

We are assured by the spiritual teacher, White Eagle, that the destruction of the soul is actually a very rare occurrence. It happens only when the deteriorating soul involved turns away resolutely from every effort made to help it to resume its path. Powerful stratagems are applied so that the soul might find its feet again, and every available strand of aid from every kingdom, from the insect world to the highest angelic realm, is summoned by Sandalphon and Michael, the two supreme angels who are associated with the guardian angel allied to every soul. The guardian angel, under the instruction of these two mighty ones, and the great zodiacal angel to which it is linked, puts out an SOS, and all that can be done, without trespassing against free will, is put into action to call the soul back to safety. If it chooses destruction, then its decision must be respected by its guardian angel, who sorrows after its lost charge.

When a soul destroys itself, the little individual spark of spirit is never destroyed. It lives on, and begins once again to unfold its gifts of divine potential. It puts forth a new garment, a new soul; and that new-born soul, assisted by the angels and many other divine beings, begins to develop all the subtle bodies belonging to its higher and lower mind (its supernal intelligence), those higher and lower expressions of the love that created it and is its essence, until, when it is ready and the time is appointed, it finally descends into an earthly vehicle of flesh. There, in the imprisoning restrictions of materialism, the soul creates a mirror-self, which is us as we experience life and consciousness on earth. Yet, do we not look deep into that mirror and sense that we are so much more than that little mirror-reflection which seems to be ourselves, and yet is, we know, only the shadow of an infinitely greater being that is held in the thrall and limitations of matter?

And do we not long for release, to be consumed in the heart of the divine fire which sent us forth on our protracted journey that spans cosmic dimensions, and then to step out of the fire, gifted at last with the knowledge of who we truly are? This is the journey and destiny of the soul – the soul that our guardian angel has been appointed to awaken, protect and guide, so that its steps might truly lead back home.

This ineffable and majestic procession of the soul answers the question as to why we have guardian angels; and the inner process of opening our interior eyes and ears that the art of meditation facilitates, so that we might not remain in spiritual penury and entrapment but rather follow after our beautiful and inspiring angelic guide, cannot be overestimated in its importance.

Guide to Meditation

The best way to consider meditation is as a wonderful treat, a precious gift we give to ourselves. It is our special time, where we are protected from the demands, frustrations and the general invasion of ordinary earthly conditions. It is a time when we go within and allow ourselves just to be, instead of feeling hounded by the usual tendency to burn our energy in 'doing'.

Because of this tendency, meditation can seem quite nebulous to the beginner! In our culture, which discourages the use of the imagination, activity is considered in terms of what is bustling and busy and outwardly productive. The idea that the attainment of complete stillness of mind and body is an activity seems to the modern materialistic mind a complete absurdity; and the further suggestion that there is a life deep within our consciousness far more vital, significant and beautiful than that of the self-important, domineering and organizing intellect outrages its narrow belief-system. Yet, if we are to create a sane world and a universal human response to values which create happiness, peace, soul-fulfilment and a kindly and even-handed society, we need to make this leap of faith, not in blindness but by observing the fruits which come forth from this most profound and powerful activity.

Proper meditation, practised with regularity and discipline, can transform a life. The insights we gain, the health of mind and body we receive, and the daily renewal of soul and spirit which is the blessing of meditation will guide and revivify us in every waking and sleeping moment. Meditation is a cup that never runs dry. The art of meditation may seem elusive at first. You are sitting there doing absolutely nothing, absolutely nothing is happening, and there are a least a hundred things which you need to do, or would rather be doing, than sitting there trying to actively do nothing. This is the lower mind, or the everyday intellect, speaking to you, and it will do everything in its power to persuade you that meditation is a foolish idea, or that you can try again tomorrow, or next week, or any time that is not now (it always is 'now', of course!).

The lower mind has the tendency to drive us like cattle. It knows instinctively that once you begin to regularly contact your higher mind, it is seriously going to lose status, and so it will fight frantically to gain ascendancy over your decision to meditate, filling you with feelings of urgency, guilt and frustration to 'act' and not just sit there. It will transmit to you all kinds of illusions that you simply cannot meditate and that meditation feels uncomfortable and unpleasant.

Just ignore its ranting, and remember that all its impressions are pure illusion. Meditation is real, and the nagging voice of the lower self will soon be silenced by your quiet decision to continue with your efforts to meditate.

The guided visualizations and contemplations given in this book are intended to start you on the meditative path by stimulating your power to create images and by so doing, enter into imaginal dimensions where you will be led to archetypes of peace and healing such as the Lake of Peace, the Spiritual Mountaintop, the Gardens of the Spirit, the Sacred Cave and the Temple of the Rose. They are a form of sacred storytelling which has a purpose for the listening soul beyond mere entertainment. The famous philosopher and psychologist Carl Jung recognized that the human need for the integrating story was as urgent as the need for food, water, sleep, companionship and sex, and provided evidence that we have a soul existence as well as a physical one.

If you are unfamiliar with meditation, you may simply choose to follow the thread of the guided visualization to its end. In time,

moments will occur when you wish to pause and to follow your own
path, seeking enlightenment from the voice and the imagery of your
own spirit. This is when the real task, the true journey which is
meditation, begins.

It is simple to learn to meditate, but not easy.

**Sit comfortably with your spine upright and supported if
necessary. (If you lie down, you will almost certainly fall
asleep, which is not a form of meditation!) Place your
right ankle lightly over your left, because this seals your
energy-field, and cup your left hand in your right. At the
spiritual level, we give with our right hand and receive
with our left.**

**Having made sure you are comfortable and relaxed, begin
to focus softly on your breathing, drawing and releasing
each breath imaginally through your heart-centre (see
above).**

**As you inhale, imagine that the golden light of the spirit is
filling you. As you exhale, breathe out all the toxins, all
the troubles and disturbances, the dis-ease, from your
mind, body and emotional self.**

**Eventually, usually after a minute or two, you will find
that you are in the light and of the light, and you will naturally both give and receive the light in your breath-cycles.**

**Now think of the highest plane you can conceive of, and
give this sphere an image. Perhaps it may be the figure of
Christ or the Buddha, the Goddess or the archangel
Michael, Vishnu or Krishna, the sun or the six-pointed
star (like the Star of David but with no internal divisions),
a bright candle-flame or some other symbol meaningful to
you which symbolizes Divine Intelligence.**

**Holding this image in your mind, you may like to softly
chant the word 'Ham' on the in-breath and 'Sah' on the
out-breath. (In ancient Sanskrit, 'Ham' means 'I am' and
'Sah' means 'Higher Self' or 'Divine Spirit', 'Divine Spark'.
(See pages 29–30)**

Your everyday mind will repeatedly attempt to sabotage this process, so when it makes its assaults by trying to drag you back to outer consciousness with some mundane thought or anxious rumination, simply return your attention, with great respect and gentleness, to your chosen image and the rhythm of your breathing. Let your intruding thoughts be as boats which pass under the bridge of your mind. Don't jump onto them or watch them sail away; just let them float by. The lower mind produces a barrage of such thoughts to distract you, but some of these thoughts are also for your healing and cleansing. Gently let them go, refusing involvement or feeling-ruffles of any kind. Alternatively you may like to give these thoughts to the image of the Divine which you hold in your mind. Let them rise up, to be taken care of by the supernal spheres.

Soon you will reach a place of utter peace and calm, beneath and beyond the busy traffic of the thought-processes, the biblical 'peace which passeth all comprehension'. It is at this point that, gradually, the spiritual worlds will open up to your inner vision, and your meditational journeys will begin, perhaps only for a second or two at first. If even a split second of vision or breakthrough is beyond your reach initially, refuse the temptation to abandon meditation in disgust! Your breakthrough *will* come, the door *will* open, before long. This is incontrovertible cosmic law. It is just a matter of persistence.

The instructions above relate to classic meditation. If your meditation exercise is to be a reading-meditation, then simply follow those concerning posture as far as you can whilst ensuring that you are in a relaxed and comfortable position for reading, although it is always best to keep your spine as straight as possible. A slouching posture greatly inhibits the depth and value of a meditational experience. The act of reading, when undertaken peacefully in solitude or at least in a state of withdrawal and detachment from immediate surroundings, enables the reader to enter into a light meditative state which is all that is required to fully experience the guided visualizations given throughout this book.

When finishing a meditation, even a light reading-meditation, it is essential to protect your finer vehicles, your non-physical bodies, by sealing the chakras. These are inner gateways, power points in the physical body where we are yoked or connected to the spiritual forces without which our bodies and the whole physical sphere could not exist. To the eye of the psychic, they look like spinning discs arranged in circles of petals like a rapidly rotating flower. In fact they are perfect representations of circular galaxies, which are also shaped like a spinning disc, with their stars and satellites and planets arrayed like the bright circling petals of a flower.

(Some galaxies are spiral in shape, beautifully reminiscent of the shape of ammonites and seashells. The disc is an ancient symbol of the masculine spiritual principle, whereas spirals have always been associated with the sacred feminine.) It is interesting to consider what galaxies might actually be in the divine scheme of things, and, perhaps, to glean a clue as to why the idea of a garden is sacred to all mythical and religious traditions, and is often given a cosmic dimension within them.

There are many chakras (see above), but the seven main 'stargates' we need to seal after meditation or any other spiritual exercise are situated in our corporeal body at the crown, the mid-brow, the hollow of the throat, the heart, the solar plexus, the spleen and the base of the spine. Imagine a vivid silver cross in a circle of light and seal each centre with this symbol (place it at mid-point upon the chakra) as soon as you emerge from meditation.

In most cases you will only need to seal the first five chakras (crown, brow, throat, heart and solar plexus). If you have entered very deeply into the experience, it will be necessary to seal all seven. You can also ground yourself by stamping both feet lightly on the ground (if you do it heavily you will shock your centres), holding the thumb and forefinger of the right hand together and saying firmly on the in-breath 'I am' and on the out-breath 'present'. Do this three times.

It is customary in many cultures to dedicate the fruits of meditation to all sentient beings. When you make this your declared intention before meditating, your gift increases in spiritual amplification and becomes a dewdrop – or even a wave – of the great ocean of divine light which humanity is creating around the earth as it sends forth radiance from its united heart-centre. One day, this great tide of heart-light will come rolling in, inundating and transforming the sullen and sinister tide of darkness that currently oppresses the Earth and her children.

CHAPTER THREE

COMMUNING WITH OUR GUARDIAN ANGEL

Part Two

Prayer

We should never underestimate the power of prayer! In particular, prayer is a beautiful way to open the process of communion with our guardian angel. Prayer creates a bond with our angel which becomes a strong, clear and protected channel for conscious communication. When we make gifts to our guardian angel, and to the angelic brotherhood, by giving forth the Prayer for Humanity at noon, or any of the other magical hours (3, 6, 9 and 12), the potency of our prayer is increased if we consciously summon our guardian angel to add its power of prayer to our own.

When we pray with our guardian angel, we do not ask anything for ourselves, except, of course, for blessings, protection, and spiritual help and guidance. If we demand anything at a materialistic or selfish level, we run the risk of activating the dark principalities of the universe, who do not give freely or for our greatest good. This does not mean that we should never ask Divine Spirit or our angels for help in specific areas, just that we should never employ our desire-nature in prayer by demanding selfishly. It is always safest, however, to end any prayer where we have asked for something specific with the words, 'Only if this accords with Divine Will, may it be so.'

More beautiful and effective than any prayer for ourselves is the dynamism of prayer when we use it to bless others, on the humblest or the grandest scale. The individual is naturally sustained and strengthened by such prayer. The following selection of prayers may be used for connecting with our guardian angel; but, of course, prayers that you word yourself will always carry their own special effectiveness. Nevertheless, the repetition of a favoured prayer becomes a calming, reassuring and lovely experience.

GREAT BRIGHT SPIRIT OF THE OPEN SPACES

Great Bright Spirit of the open spaces,

the mountaintops and the peaceful valleys;

Great Bright Spirit of nature,

and of the heavens above the earth,

and of the waters beneath;

Great Bright Spirit of eternity, infinity,

we are enfolded within thy great heart.

We rest our heart upon thy heart.

Great Father and Mother God,

we love, we worship thee;

we resign all into thy loving keeping,

knowing that thou art love,

and that all moves forward

into the light.

White Eagle (From *Prayer in the New Age*)

THE GUARDIAN ANGEL

**(Adapted from a prayer traditional to the Western Isles
of Scotland)**

Thou Guardian Angel who hast charge of me

Sent by the mercy of the Great Spirit,

Encompass me in thy circle of perfect light,

Enfold me in thy fragrant wings.

Drive from me every temptation and danger,

Surround me on the sea of unrighteousness,

And in the narrows, crooks and straits,

Keep thou my coracle, keep it always.

Be thou a bright flame before me,

Be thou a guiding star above me,

Be thou a smooth path below me,

And be a kindly shepherd behind me,

Today, tonight, and for ever.

Lead thou me to the land of angels;

Lead thou me to my true and radiant home,

To the Court of the Lightener of the Stars,

To the white peace of heaven.

CELTIC BLESSING

Deep peace of the running wave to you,

Deep peace of the flowing air to you,

Deep peace of the quiet earth to you,

Deep peace of the shining stars to you,

Deep peace of the Son of Peace to you...

Peace between nations,

Peace between neighbours,

Peace between lovers,

In love of the God of life.

Peace between religions,

Peace between world-views,

Peace between differences,

In love of the God of life.

Peace between races,

Peace between man and earth,

Peace between man and beasts,

In love of the God of life.

Peace between person and person,

Peace between wife and husband,

Peace between parent and child.

In love of the God of life.

The peace of Heaven above all peace.

Bless O Heaven our hearts

Let our hearts incessantly bless,

Bless O Heaven our faces,

Let our faces bless one and all,

Bless O Heaven our eyes,

Let our eyes bless everything they see...

**(From the *Carmina Gadelica*, collected and edited by
Alexander Carmichael)**

THE TWENTY-THIRD PASLM

The Lord is my shepherd; I shall not want.

He maketh me to lie down in green pastures: he
leadeth me beside the still waters.

He restoreth my soul:

he leadeth me in the paths of righteousness for his
name's sake.

Yea, though I walk through the valley of the shadow of
death,

I will fear no evil: for thou art with me;

thy rod and thy staff they comfort me.

Thou preparest a table before me in the presence of
mine enemies:

thou anointest my head with oil; my cup runneth over.

Surely goodness and mercy shall follow me

all the days of my life:

and I will dwell in the house of the Lord forever.

(The Old Testament: The Book of Psalms)

SON OF THE SKY LOOM

O our Mother the Earth, O our Father the Sky,

Your children are we, and with tired backs

We bring you the gifts you love.

Then weave for us a garment of brightness;

May the warp be the white light of morning,

May the weft be the red light of evening,

May the fringes be the falling rain,

May the border be the standing rainbow.

So weave for us a garment of brightness,

That we may walk fittingly where birds sing,

That we may walk fittingly where grass is green,

O our Mother the Earth, O our Father the Sky

(Tewa Indian prayer – nineteenth century, USA)

PRAYER TO BRIGID

O Brigid of beauteous spirit, of the tender shining
Light,

Encompass me in your wings of flame, in your kindly
fire;

Let my heart open and release the fragrance of the
Rose;

Let Love be my comfort, my gift and my guiding star.

INVOCATION TO BRIGID'S ANGELIC ESSENCE

Brigid the Bright, Brigid the White, Divine
Shepherdess;

overlight my life

and draw me into your radiant presence.

Increase my compassion

and let healing flow forth from me.

May I ever breathe your holy breath

so that the life force blesses and burns bright in me;

and put your mystic flame in my heart

so that I might always express the poetry of my being

and the songs within my soul,

whatever form these might take, humble or glorious.

In love and light I offer thanks

to the Angel Brigid.

PRAYER TO DIVINE MOTHER
AND HER ANGELS

Since you are the star of ocean,

Pilot me at sea.

Since you are the star of earth,

Guide me on land.

Since you are the star of night,

Lighten me in the darkness.

Since you are the sun of day,

Encompass me on land.

Since you are the star of angels,

Watch over me on earth.

Since you are the star of Paradise,

Companion me to heaven.

Be you my safeguarding by night

Be you my safeguarding by day,

Be you my safeguarding both day and night,

You bright and kindly queen of heaven.

**(From the *Carmina Gadelica*,
collected and edited by Alexander Carmichael)**

ANGEL PRAYER FOR HEALING THE EARTH

We call on the Archangel Raphael,

the Earth Angel Sophia,

and all the Healing Angels,

to bring healing to our beloved Mother Earth.

We send forth the golden starlight from our own
human hearts

to penetrate, bless and heal the Earth,

her animals, and her world of Nature and its spirits;

and to speed and ground the healing rays

manifested by the angels.

We send forth the golden starlight from our hearts

to heal and bless all humanity.

We pray for the upliftment of every member of
humankind

into the spheres of harmony

and perfect spiritual attunement

which resonate between the Earth and her human
children.

Amen.

DAGARA PRAYER

May our ancestors breathe blessing

onto us for our eyes to open,

and our life purpose to become clear.

**(from *Of Water and the Spirit*,
by Malidoma Patrice Somé)**

PRAYER TO THE ANGEL OF THE MORNING

Radiant Angel of the Morning,

who sings to me through the song of the birds

and caresses my soul through the play of the new-born
light,

throw your glorious garment of love around the Earth,

around her human children,

her animal children,

and all her world of nature and its spirits;

and bless the chalice within our hearts

which receives the spiritual sunlight.

See the Angel's garment shining over all the world like a scintillating star, and accept the Angel's gift of joy.

PRAYER TO THE ANGEL OF THE EVENING

Beautiful Angel of the Evening,

who calls to my soul through the farewell songs of the
birds,

and the love-lament of the fading light,

and the softly-stealing dusk,

wrap your mantle of protection around the Earth this
night,

around her human children,

her animal children,

and all her world of nature and its spirits;

and bless the footfalls of the Lightener of the Stars.

See the angel's mantle being drawn in protection around all the
world like a great ring of light containing a bright golden cross, and
accept the angel's gift of peace.

MICHAEL, THE VICTORIOUS

Thou Michael the victorious,

I make my circuit under thy shield,

Thou Michael of the white steed,

And of the bright brilliant blades,

Conqueror of the dragon,

Be thou at my back,

Thou ranger of the heavens,

Thou warrior of the King of all

O Michael the victorious,

My pride and my guide,

O Michael the victorious,

The glory of mine eye.

I make my circuit

In the fellowship of my saint,

By the water, on the meadow,

On the cold heathery hill;

Though I should traverse oceans

And the hard globe of the world

No harm can e'er befall me

'Neath the shelter of thy shield;

O Michael the victorious,

Jewel of my heart,

O Michael the victorious,

God's shepherd thou art.

**(From the *Carmina Gadelica*,
collected and edited by Alexander Carmichael)**

GUARDIAN ANGEL INVOCATION FOR THE CLOSE OF DAY

Thou angel of God who hast charge of me

From the fragrant Mother and Father of mercifulness,

The gentle encompassing of the Sacred Heart

To make round my soul-shrine this night,

Oh, round my soul-shrine this night.

Ward from me every distress and danger,

Encompass my course over the ocean of truth,

I pray thee, place thy pure light before me,

O bright beauteous angel on this very night,

Bright beauteous angel on this very night.

Be Thyself the guiding star above me,

Illume Thou to me every reef and shoal,

Pilot my barque on the crest of the wave,

To the restful haven of the waveless sea,

Oh, the restful haven of the waveless sea.

**(From the *Carmina Gadelica*, collected and edited by
Alexander Carmichael)**

The following prayer is a prayer to the angels, and in particular to the guardian angel, said on rising, or first waking, in the morning. The 'kindling' is the holy breath (your own breath, given to you by the Godhead and called in many traditions 'celestial fire') breathing upon the flame of spirit in your heart, which will link you consciously with the Divine, one aspect of which is your guardian angel. With this prayer, you attune yourself in entirety to the angelic sphere and to your encompassing by your guardian angel.

BLESSING OF THE KINDLING
(MORNING PRAYER)

I will kindle my fire this morning

In presence of the holy angels in heaven,

In presence of the holy angel by my side

Who is also my shepherd behind me,

In presence of Ariel of the loveliest form,

In presence of Uriel of the myriad charms,

Without malice, without jealousy, without envy,

Without fear, without terror of any one under the sun,

But the Holy Child of Light to shield me.

Goddess-God, kindle Thou in my heart within

A flame of love to my neighbour,

To my foe, to my friend, to my kindred all,

To the brave, to the knave, to the thrall,

O Child of the pure and lovely Mother,

O Child of the Divine Mother,

From the lowliest thing that liveth,

To the Name that is highest of all.

O Child of the pure and loveliest Mother,

O Child of the Divine Mother,

To the Name that is highest of all.

**(From the *Carmina Gadelica*, collected and edited by
Alexander Carmichael)**

ANGELIC SEED-THOUGHTS

This is the secret
You have shared with Your angels:
'The honey is worth the sting.'

Rumi

The angels keep their ancient places; -
Turn but a stone and start a wing!
'Tis ye, 'tis your estrang-ed faces,
That miss the many-splendoured thing.

Francis Thompson

Heaven white with angels' wings,
Earth and the white-waved sea.

Medieval Irish poem

Ask, and it shall be given you.
Seek, and ye shall find.
Knock, and it shall be opened to you.
For whoever asks, receives;
And he who seeks, finds;
And to him who knocks,
The door is opened.

(Matthew 7:7-8)

'Pray inwardly, even if you do not enjoy it.
It does good though you feel nothing, see nothing.
'Yes, even though you think you are doing nothing.
'For when you are dry, empty, sick, or weak,
at such time is your prayer most pleasing to me,
though you find little enough to enjoy in it.'

(The words of God, received by
the female medieval mystic, Julian of Norwich)

Aspire to the heavens through prayer,
for as true prayer is expressed in the human heart,
it rises like incense into the heavens,
and calls from the heavens
the response that the soul cries for.

White Eagle

Heart-to-Heart Communion

Although we can consciously link with our guardian angel at any time, and may choose to allot a certain period each day for this purpose alone, in my experience the guardian angel, of its own volition, communicates with us most clearly just before we drift off to sleep at night, and in those moments of serene clarity after we have woken from sleep, but have not yet quite stepped onto the shores of everyday waking consciousness. At these special times, and whenever you make conscious contact with your angel, your communion will deepen into its fullest potential if you first make the firm decision to entirely open your heart, without reservation, inhibition, shame or denial.

We all have a wounded, shadow self that terrifies us, and that we can hardly bear to face full on. It is certainly no part of our angel's intention to scourge us, or to force us to identify with those darker, disturbing climes of our soul that distress us.

Indeed, our angel will always gently and resolutely verify that the darkness which clings to us is not a true part of our real self, as if it said, 'This darkness does not really belong to you, dear friend. It is a trespasser, and together we will heal and transform it so that it serves your soul.' It is a negative act to deny our shadow self, and thus to create blind spots in our perception, with all their hazardous and even highly dangerous implications. Trusting and confiding in our guardian angel will gently ease us into the confidence we need to reveal all to our angel.

Think of yourself as a wise and kindly overseer of your own soul-temple – your life as you live it, and as its dynamics touch others. There is a much greater aspect to the soul-temple than that encompassed by the description just given. Nevertheless, our earthly life is the key to everything, and the time and attention we give to its spiritual import and repercussions, heart-to-heart with our guardian angel, is of the utmost value.

As we confidently open our heart to our angel, we will find that it puts clear images into our thoughts of straitened areas within us that need our attention – things we are doing or thoughts we are thinking that do not resonate with our spiritual reality, and are thus doing harm to ourselves or others (including our environment and our animal brethren). Our compassion and concern will be awakened, but we must beware of remorse. Let us keep remorse strictly within moderate bounds, and transmute it into a wise and balanced desire to make good the problem. Anything more brings hopelessness and paralysis of our creative energies. The dark, adversarial forces use shame to make us feel disempowered and incapable of change, and utilize the taunts of shame and self-blame to force us to quickly re-establish our blind spots and denial as the only means of procuring a tolerable state of inner peace.

Rebuke or chastisement plays no part in our angel's response to us. In fact, as it deepens its understanding of your earthly self, its love will be able to run into ever more profound channels, and you will feel an inrush of sound, warm support. It will never condemn, or think less of us because of anything that lurks in our lower nature. Its love is infinite and unchanging; but our angel does rejoice when we strive to bring into harmony that which is brought to our perception as out of balance. Your guardian angel has every confidence in you, and does indeed regard you as that 'wise and kindly overseer of your own soul-temple' stated above. It brings disharmony and straitness to your attention because it trusts absolutely, and indeed can clearly see, that you have the strength and integrity and beauty of heart to heal them. When you work with your guardian in this way, you are veritably doing angel's work – smoothing a crumple and a jagged edge here, removing a stain and an impediment there, and gradually restoring your soul-temple to wholesomeness and harmonious order.

The time for you and your guardian angel to take counsel together this way will generally be late at night and in the morning, just before and after sleep. Your times of communion during the day will not, generally, concentrate on adjustment, but are more likely to encompass the joy and the positive power generated by sharing your hopes and aspirations with your angel, or experiencing the solace and renewed confidence it brings to you in full measure when you share with your angel friend the inevitable disappointments and rebuffs that life deals out along our way.

Adjustment is not the only task that your angel will carry out for you in your receptive times between sleeping and waking, of course. There will be many revelations, solutions to problems, wonderfully inspired ideas and suggestions. However certainly you imagine you will hold them clearly in memory, you will almost definitely forget them completely by the time you rise the next day. The earthly memory begrudges fidelity to the spiritual memory!

Because of this, it is essential to keep a notebook and pen by your bed. Everything that comes lucidly and beautifully into your mind between waking and sleeping, and sleeping and waking, is from either your angel or your spirit guide, who works hand in hand with your angel to help you. Take care not to waste this treasury of inspiration and guidance. If you do not record it and take no notice of it, the sensitivity of the channel through which you receive it will eventually dull and deafen. Angels do not put effort and energy into projects of which we refuse to make use. They are divine economists!

Keep vividly in mind that your communion with your guardian angel must always be heart-to-heart. Make full use of the instructions and exercises given to lead you to your heart-centre, and to find the point of silence, peace and stillness there within; but it is important to remember that opening your heart to your angel is an act that proceeds from your will and consent. Exercises and instruction can prepare the way, but have no power to force the issue. That power lies only with you and your intention.

If you find that, against your wishes, you have problems in opening up your heart-centre with ease and confidence, you may find that the information given in the next chapter will bring you healing and resolution.

Grounding

It is preferable to be grounded before beginning to communicate with your guardian angel, because you will feel more in control of your thoughts and your perception. This makes it easier to receive what comes to you from your angel, and removes any vague or inchoate element from your responses.

- Imagine strong, wholesome roots growing from the soles
  of your feet and anchoring themselves deep into the
  essence of Mother Earth.

- Another method is to hold a grounding crystal
  (previously cleansed – just hold it under the flow of the
  cold tap for a second or two) such as a bloodstone, an
  obsidian, or a smoky quartz in your left hand for a few
  moments until you feel steadied and centred.

- A third way is to affirm on the in-breath, aloud and
  whilst holding your right thumb and forefinger together,
  'I am', and on the out-breath, 'present'. Do this three
  times.

- A fourth way is to gently become aware of your cycles of breath, and then to see a thread of bright golden light coming up from under your left foot and up your left side to encircle your body seven times. Then, from the star chakra, which shines at your crown, just above your head, pull a ramrod of light straight down through the middle of your being and right into your earth-star chakra, which is located a little distance below your feet. Thus the great Sword of Light balances and correctly connects heaven and earth for you. You can try this method on days when you are feeling dreamy or floaty, and your thoughts are particularly disobedient.

- If you experience days when your energies feel severely unsettled, a little time spent in gardening (especially digging) or walking in nature will help you. And it is always worth calling on the angels of the earth element to stabilize and earth such chaotic energies.

Chanting

The Sufi mystic Hazrat Inayat Khan has written, 'Divine sound is the cause of all manifestation. The knower of the mystery of sound knows the mystery of the whole universe.' The uterus is so called because it is the sacred vessel for life, the 'utterer' of the Divine Word. It is believed that the ancient and secret Essene brotherhood at Qumran protected their community from hostile interference by employing the mystery of 'the Sound', by which means their enemies were harmlessly – but conclusively – kept at bay. The magical 'aum' is said to be the heartbeat of the universe.

Chanting, whilst holding the word or the sound peacefully in our heart-centred awareness, is a powerful means of communing with our guardian angel, and our angelic group. Here are four simple suggestions for chants:

Angel Invocation

The first chant was given to humanity by an angel. It was initially presented in Alma Daniel, Timothy Wyllie and Andrew Ramer's excellent book, *Ask Your Angels**. Say the words in a slow, even rhythm, letting your mind focus gently on their meaning.

Eee Nu Rah

Eee Nu Rah

Eee Nu Rah

Zay

Eee – I bring all of me that transcends the physical body
Nu – my physical body
Rah – my soul
Zay – together in the company of the angels.

When we wish to resonate with a certain quality, and to take it deep within ourselves, we can chant the word that denotes the quality we desire. Our guardian angel will summon the angel which expresses that quality throughout the mystery of its being and add its own power and poignancy to the quality we wish to absorb.

Chant the word to invoke the angel:

Peace	*Joy*	*Swiftness*
Love	*Forgiveness*	*Release*
Wisdom	*Humour*	*Enlightenment*
Healing	*Beauty*	*Harmony*

The list is endless, of course. However, be warned – if you invoke a quality that does not vibrate in harmony with the higher mind and the radiant soul, creatures other than – and very different to – denizens of the angelic kingdom will be called upon to produce it!

A simple but powerful chant is the Aramaic word *Maranatha* (all

Ask Your Angels: A Practical Guide to Working With Angels to Enrich Your Life, Piatkus 1992

its syllables have a drawn-out 'ah' sound). It means 'Come, Lord, come!' ('I receive Thee'). It is an invitation for consciousness of an exalted frequency or vibration to mingle with our own and carry us to the supernal realms of the soul.

The vowels themselves, in many holy literatures, are held to be sacred. The angels have verified that these sounds contain mighty creative power. To the five vowel sounds should be added the sound of manifestation: the 'Ah'; and the sound of completeness: the 'om'.

A

E

I

O

U

AH

OM

Singing

The angels of music draw close when we sing, or create, or listen to, music. They can pour into you creative power, which enables you to better express the music of your own soul. Our guardian angel loves to hear us sing, when through song we aim to raise our vibrations.

Dancing

When we dance upon the earth and truly express joy, our angels draw very close to us.

The joy of dancing has been forgotten, except by those remote tribes who still remember the happiness, rising to ecstasy, the healing, and the fostering and restoration of grounded sanity that free and expressive dancing brings to us. We should not be hampered and restricted by the narrow, artificial forms our dancing has assumed in the West, so full of ego and social convention. We can all dance! Dancing under the stars is particularly inspiring, as shall be discussed later.

Art, Literature, Music, Poetry

Attuning ourselves to the realms of all forms of art facilitates angelic communion. It stimulates the right side of the brain, where once we possessed organs of inner perception that have now atrophied. Listening often to beautiful music, and learning and reading poetry, facilitates angelic communion, as does the study of art and the sensitive, attuned absorption of pure colours. Reading literature in which truth, beauty, creativity, and higher-vibrational thoughts are expressed, also lifts us into the realms of the angels.

Birdsong

The notes of birdsong are akin to the angelic language as it was revealed to Enoch the prophet. Listen closely to birdsong and you will begin to receive angelic messages.

Ancient lore, and the prophets and teachers that inspired it, tell us that birdsong is magical. There is a mystical link between angels and birds, and the language of the one mirrors the language of the other. Birdsong is a lower harmonic of the songs of the angels; and angel language is much more than a means of communication. It is the means by which, via the divine inflow from the great Source of all, creation in its entirety is harmoniously sung or spoken into being. Mythologies and religious texts worldwide refer at some point to this deeply sacred singing or 'Word' which breathes the universe into being.

Although this power streams forth from the divine imagination of Goddess-God or Cosmic Intelligence, it is the angels themselves who minister to the manifestation of the divine imagination, creating evolving form and ensouling it with ever more beautiful and rarefied essence as that material form progressively becomes a perfected receptacle for such essence.

Within each member of humankind, it is said, the whole of the cosmos is reflected in microcosm. Therefore, these vibrations, which so mysteriously create and bring into being, are present in the depths of each human soul. The resonances of birdsong play upon this

magical harp of Apollo or Orpheus within us and draw forth vibrations which in turn respond to sacred influences from the heavenly
worlds.

To draw close to the birds in spirit, to listen with an open heart
to their cascades of song and to attune the soul to their joyous out-
pourings, is a poignantly beautiful way to embrace the angelic
streams of life. Through their association with the angels, birds can
teach us of the hidden beauties and mysteries which are secreted
within the human soul. They bring us teachings about our own soul
and the soul of all creation. They bear messages from the heavenly
worlds, and through their flight, their songs and their presence, they
open a doorway to the spheres of the spirit and lift us in our light
bodies up into airy heights of invigorating sweetness.

One way that we can attune to these soul aspects, these special
soul qualities which are like buried treasure within us, is to listen so
closely to their calls that we can begin to imitate them. In my experience, birds are most responsive to our bird-like human calls in the
early evening, before the approach of twilight. Single strains of
birdsong are much easier to identify at this time, and take on a
melodious richness and poignancy which delights and awakens the
heart-intelligence. It is then that we can enter into antiphony with
them.

With practice and patience, taking care to keep our communion
heart-centred, we will find that the birds call back in answer to us.
Half an hour spent in enjoying such a pastime will have a truly
magical effect on all the subtle vehicles within us. We will feel
centred in peace, and as if we can gaze into limitless worlds inside
our soul which scintillate with an exquisite radiance. Our soul will
unfold unearthly wings and teach us that no prison, no chains either
mental or physical can ever contain or bind us. We will know that
we are free.

I am quite convinced that birds meditate, or, to be more
accurate, are firmly attuned to the meditative rhythm of creation, in
which the all-pervading Breath of the indwelling Spirit is constantly
drawn within, and then given out. Listening to the colonies of birds
in my garden, I have noticed that, without fail, their songs and

chirrups follow a pattern of prolonged bursts, followed by a moment or two of complete silence. After four or five seconds, a few birdcalls sound the signal that the rest period is over, and the chorus starts up again – only to die away entirely a little while later, and then to resume in the same vein. The rhythm is continuous and never-failing. Does this apply only to the birds in my garden?! I can hardly believe this to be so. I can only state that, whether it is universal, or peculiar only to the birds that I listen to daily, there is a form of communal meditation going on!

Throughout myth and folktale, birds intervene dramatically in the life of human beings. In poetry and literature, their secret significance comes to light again and again. W B Yeats refers to them many times throughout his work. In 'Paudeen', he tells the story of his exasperation with a prosaic, small-minded shopkeeper 'until a curlew cried, and in the luminous wind, / a curlew answered'; and it was borne to him that in the truth and the vision of the spiritual worlds, high above the confusion and distortions of the earth, 'There cannot be… a single soul that lacks a sweet crystalline cry'; and the poet's heart was restored to the holistic vision of a world where all creatures sound their own note of beauty throughout creation. And in 'A Memory of Youth', he tells how, although love had its earthly expression in the usual rapport between a man and a woman, which is enough for youth, its spiritual face or presence eventually became hidden away by 'a cloud from the north', or the colder climes of human nature; and how he and his lover would thus have been 'savagely undone', 'Were it not that Love upon the cry / Of a most ridiculous little bird / Tore from the clouds his most marvellous moon.'

Go profoundly inside the sound of birdsong and find the point of silence within its pulsations, the potent stillness beneath the notes. If, by an act of your spiritual will, you can exclude all invasive noise except these hallowed sounds and silences, you will begin to hear the symphony of life itself moving through your being, the songs of the angels themselves as they sustain creation in its forward motion, in its grand cycles and great sacred spiral. The birds can give you this gift of revelation. They can tear from the clouds of dimmed spiritual vision 'Love's most marvellous moon'. They can embody heavenly qualities with the sound of their songs and link you via the stairway of these sacred sounds directly to the heart of the Great Spirit.

In order to celebrate the angel and the god within us, we too need to be constantly surrounded by the soul-energies of birds. We can ensure that we are by regularly attuning ourselves to the harmonies of birdsong and to the joy and mystery of their presence, seeking to understand them and their angel-inspired language.

—⌒ **A N G E L I C   S E E D - T H O U G H T** ⌒—

He who bend to himself a joy,
Doth the winged life destroy.
But he who kisses a joy as it flies
Lives in eternity's sunrise.

William Blake

CHAPTER FOUR

THE SECRET OF THE ROSE, THE STAR, AND THE GOLDEN FLOWER

At the end of this chapter, a meditation is given which will help you to consciously meet with your guardian angel, and thereby enter into deep communion with it.

Before this important initiation takes place, we will, via meditation, or, more correctly, guided visualization, explore three of the deepest secrets of the heart. In attuning ourselves sensitively to these mysteries via the imagination, we will be better able to embrace the presence of our guardian angel.

The Spirit of the Rose

A profound mystery resides in the emblem of the rose blooming at the very heart of the cross which is matter's innermost secret. For the rose is a sign for the heart and for human and divine love; and when it blooms upon the cross of matter in the individual life so that the spiritual essence pervades the earthly being, that man or woman in esoteric lore is seen to be 'Christed', to be expressing the divine life. In contemplating the rose, we may directly comprehend the mysteries, perhaps only in glyphs and glimpses as our limited vision permits, but yet also by means of cosmic apperception because the rose is such a potent symbol, able to raise the soul above the confines of earthly understanding. At the heart of every rose is a circle of golden stamens. It is a sigil, written in matter itself, of the 'mind in the heart', that seat of consciousness which is not the head-mind of everyday awareness, or the limited, calculating, ego-rooted intellect, but rather the intuition, that point of intelligence which bears the gifts of inner seeing and spiritual percipience, and within which can be found the true self.

It is said that a few minutes spent each day in meditation upon the heart of a rose will heal human ills and soothe every conflict and vexation of the spirit; that there is a power and an essence distilled by the rose which is beyond all earthly understanding. Perhaps this is why Dante's highest vision was of the Celestial Rose of Paradise.

It is not always possible to meditate upon the heart of an actual rose. Yet we can always enter the heart of the mystical rose, and partake of the deep healing peace which is its essence, remembering always that the rose dwells within us, within our heart-centre, and is our very heart of hearts. From that innermost sanctuary, we can breathe forth the Spirit of the Rose.

Meditation – The Spirit of the Rose

Sit comfortably, spine upright, supported if necessary, and breathe quietly and easily, a little deeper than usual. Find your heart-centre by attuning to the star which shines so beautifully there.

Bring before your mind's eye the image of a rose in full bloom. Our rose for this meditation is a pink rose, a deep pink like the first flush of sunrise.

Think of the perfect form and structure of the rose, the soft radiance of its colour, its mystical perfume, the velvet and silk of its fragrant flesh.

A rose is a being, a messenger from the angelic domains, visiting earth to teach us of the wisdom, the truth, the beauty, the peace and the transcendent joy of life. The note upon which it is called forth into being sounds from the heart.

Begin now to lay aside the garment of the physical body. Feel the buoyancy and airiness of your shining soul-body as it quickens with divine life, divine freedom.

Your rose is before you like a light-filled temple formed from the mystic proportions of its glowing pink petals, a mandala calling you to go within.

Step into the rose, into that secret exquisite chamber. There is a pure and gentle radiance here, a tender and lovely power in the texture and composition of this rose temple. Sweetest of all is the enfolding fragrance, the rapturous perfume which is the spirit of the rose.

Touch the walls of the temple of the rose; kneel and touch the floor. It is like touching a welcoming hand, warm and loving, flesh made perfect, made divine.

There is a source from which the radiance, the perfume, the body and the architecture of this sanctified being flows forth. Press deeper into the cave of the rose temple, walk on into its very heart.

Here at the sacred heart of the rose a precious, priceless jewel is shining. Lovely and beloved is that jewel so that your spirit dances as you behold it. Know that the jewel *is* your spirit, the laughing, singing golden and silver flame alight in your heart and in the heart of all humanity.

In wonder you watch as a golden door opens into the jewel.

Marvelling, you step through this shining entrance into a chamber of rainbow light. At its centre is a seat of purest white light from which these seven lovely hues emanate.

There sits Divine Mother, Goddess of the Rose, smiling and welcoming you to her. In delight and adoration, you sit down at her feet and look up into her radiance to find that in her left hand she holds a distaff and is spinning, and with her right hand she is weaving...

Folds and folds of the most delicate cloth fall away from her as she spins and weaves. It has a shimmering lustre, made as if by a flame dancing at the heart of a half-transparent pearl, and a swansdown quality, like the silk of a spider.

The magical rays of the rainbow play on and through it, for they are a living part of its weft. Sometimes it seems as you watch that shadows and mists gather, and darkness is woven into the cloth; but then you realize that the darkness always reveals a breathtaking treasury of brilliant stars.

In deepening wonder, you realize that Divine Mother is spinning and weaving the course of every human life down below so that the cloth contains a firmament of unfolding lives in its pattern.

You can see that some souls encounter horrors and griefs that seem too great to be borne, and that these experiences make the darkness in Divine Mother's cloth. Yet you see also that the arms of Divine Mother enclose every soul unfailingly and always catch them as they fall; and that the arms of the Heavenly Father reach down to lift them into worlds of light.

Then the darkness melts away and is no more, for it cannot touch the children of Divine Mother and Heavenly Father. It has no real existence or dominion, and only descends for a measured time, until the bright star it secretes within its bosom is revealed to the encountering soul.

All this you see and realize in the comforting shelter of Divine Mother, Goddess of the Rose; and deep within, where your heart's flame is one with hers, you know that all is well, and that all manner of things shall be well.

As you sit at her feet, peacefully aware that your gentle breathing and the soothing rhythm of your heart draw their sustenance from Divine Mother, you see her heart-centre magically open like a golden flower which enfolds you so that you are drawn inside.

You realize once again that you are in the heart of the Mystical Rose, cradled in golden light, hushed by the sweetness of Creative Silence which lifts you on the swell of its grand symphony. Heavenly perfume surrounds you and becomes your breath.

As a child opening its eyes in the sunflood of the morning, you see that all the universe is a sphere, a perfect sphere of time, space and matter, kept perpetually in motion by the inconceivable fire which is the breath, the heartbeat of God. And this sphere of matter revolves in the very heart of God, separated only by a mist of its own unknowing.

Released from the spell of this ignorance, you dwell in the centre of the golden light, aware that all around you is the great cosmic heart of Love.

In bliss, in peace, you rest and have your being.

Then comes the Divine Child, the Golden One, the Christ, who is the spirit of this perfect, all-enfolding love you are bathing in with such joy.

Receive the holy blessing from the Son-Daughter; breathe in this miracle of deep, deep renewal, borne on the breath of the Spirit of Love.

Know that Love is the Divine Life, the inconceivable fire, of God; and that peace is its one true receptacle, its creative channel which alone can express the glorious dynamism of the Godhead. This Love, this Peace, is given to you now.

Gently, you are led back, back to the house of your physical body, back to the waiting earth.

As you softly touch down into normal consciousness, you hear these words speaking in your heart:

'Let not your heart be troubled, nor let it be afraid.'

Seal your centres, and affirm:

I am enfolded in the Love and Peace of the Mystic Rose.

I am enfolded in the Love and Peace of the Mystic Rose

I am enfolded in the Love and Peace of the Mystic Rose.

—ᴄ   A N G E L I C   S E E D · T H O U G H T S   ᴄ—

He who would have beautiful roses in his garden
must have beautiful roses in his heart.

S Reynolds Hole (from *A Book About Roses*)

'You have a great opportunity to work for the
upliftment and spiritualization of the whole
world, and for the establishment of a universal
brotherhood in a world united and at peace...
Brotherhood can only be brought about by the
spirit of the Rose.' [and the spirit of the radiant
star within the heart, at the centre of which the
Rose dwells] 'Thus we hold up for you at this time
the symbol of the Rose, this ancient symbol of the
Brotherhood which is the symbol of the heart.'

White Eagle

The mystical rose, the star, the golden flower, the many-faceted
jewel of wondrous purity – these all dwell in the heart-centre, and
are its mysteries. They are all the heart, yet each secret wonder resonates with a power and a consciousness of its own.

The star shines at the heart-centre. The rose is its innermost
heart. Yet, the heart of the rose contains the golden flower; and the
golden flower contains the many-faceted jewel, the penetration of
which leads us into the heart of a mystery beyond words, beyond
thought; and yet we know it is our very essence, our source, and the
point to which we long to, and are bound to, return.

Now we have contemplated the mystery of the rose, we can
progress to the secret of the golden flower.

The Secret of the Golden Flower — Its Philosophical Source

The realization of the truth of the 'golden flower' has been enshrined for us in the timeless spiritual philosophy of ancient China. The religion of China has been largely misunderstood by the West. Its ancient form was a state of spiritual enlightenment which incorporated elements of the Japanese Shin-to system of perceiving divinity in nature and natural forms, and lay very close to much New Age and esoteric thinking of today.

The ancient Chinese did not worship their ancestors, but rather venerated them. They were seen as elder brethren, souls who had gone on before and had attained a higher state of evolution than those still toiling in earth lives, and who were willing to offer help and guidance to their younger brethren.

This veneration of the ancestors was not simplistic, because the Chinese understood the law of karma and reincarnation, so much so that borrowers of wealth or goods would strike deals to repay their creditors in their next life. An 'ancestor' was, properly, a soul who had transcended the need for incarnation and had ascended to the celestial worlds. The progressive spiritual concepts which we are beginning to recognize and explore today were, to the ancient Chinese, absolute and practical realities. In the earliest history of Chinese civilization, women were deeply esteemed and honoured, and the golden pheasant, the earthly representative of the divine Feng Bird, was worshipped as their symbol.

The seminal ideas of their philosophy were those of yang and yin, of manifesting spirit and law (ch'i and li), and these concepts, rooted in their spiritual vision, inspired the system of ethics evolved by the sage Confucius and the mystical thoughts of his contemporary (some say his pupil), the old master, Lao Tzu. The two are supposed to have had an interview, after which Confucius declared in exasperation that he could understand the flight of birds and the movement of fishes, but he could not understand Lao Tzu and could only compare him with the dragon!

Lao Tzu's essence is that of the enigmatic. His birth is said to have been miraculous. His teachings, the Tao or 'the Way', show us how to perceive and how to be guided by the movement of spirit through the world of matter with the entire sphere of ourselves rather than with the intellect alone, an inspiration from the feminine principle of wisdom which the more yang-overloaded, cerebral Confucius could not comprehend, so prompting him to liken Lao Tzu to the feminine dragon. In the Tao Te Ching, Lao Tzu bequeathed to the world an interpretation of that most enigmatic and profoundly subtle system of perception, the transcendental understanding embodied in the Hindu Upanishads.

Kuan Yin symbolizes the beautiful loving-kindness ethos of Buddhism and is associated with the Chinese prophecy that a female Buddha will incarnate on earth, embodying the compassionate yin force without which the yang principle becomes incapable of expressing the healing dynamism of peace.

Meditation – The Temple of the Sun

Focus on your heart-centre and concentrate on your breathing for a few moments, quietly inhaling and exhaling 'through the heart'. Ensure that your spine is straight, relaxed and comfortable, supported if necessary. Through the simple rhythm of your breath, find the point of peace within, where all is calm and tranquil.

You are walking up a gently sloping hill to the doorway of the sublime Palace of Light.

It is built of mirroring silver and flashing white gold, and is inlaid with purest pearl, white crystals and faceted diamonds. It has three tiers, and the craftsmanship of its construction is as delicate as exquisitely-wrought lace. It pulses with lustre as if it were the lightener of the stars.

At either side of the arched doorway stands a beautiful Chinese woman in traditional dress. You exchange bows with these women before entering the Palace of Light.

As you walk into its interior you feel as if you are stepping into a vast fountain of pure brightness. Through the pearly rays of light you see that at the heart of this central chamber there is a great three-tiered altar of shining white marble.

Upon the top tier a great vermilion bird, with sweeping tailfeathers and plumage of fiery beauty, sits waiting.

It is the Chinese phoenix, the mythical Feng Bird. She is as big as a small horse and sits with wings outstretched, regarding you with ocean-deep eyes, azure as blue jasper.

You kneel before the altar and dedicate the sacred flame in your heart to the spiritual source of light within the chamber, which you know is being broadcast to the world from the Palace of Light.

As soon as this is done, the mighty Feng Bird swoops to your feet. She invites you to climb on to her back so that she may become your ariel steed.

Her feathers are long and silky, beautifully soft and warm. It is easy to cling to her without fear of falling.

She rises straight up into the air, like a skylark. As you gain height, the golden Feng Bird gives forth a rapturous river of song, and you both soar into a rarefied spiritual dimension far above the astral plane you first encountered.

There is another temple here, set on a hilltop in the supernal worlds, the perfect ideation of the Palace of Light far below.

It is made of a living white substance more beautiful than any material essence, which constantly eases, cleanses and delights the soul, setting the bird of your spirit free so that it ascends and sings with the Feng Bird, who is circling the roof of the temple in ecstasy.

You see the flame in your heart dancing within your spirit-bird, and a greater, more potent flame incandescent within the Feng Bird, and you know that they are fire-birds, manifestations of divine consciousness; and you understand why, in the legends of the fire-birds, they are so precious and so sought-after.

You enter the doorway of the temple, and see within a single white rose upon an altar like a still white flame forming a chalice, white as alabaster.

A venerable Chinese sage stands before the altar. He beckons to you to come forward.

'This is the white rose of peace,' he says to you. 'You can take its perfume into your own heart and breathe it out to heal the conflict in the hearts of humanity.'

You stand before the altar and inhale the pure fragrance of the rose of peace. Within its embrace the certainty rises within you that you are a being of absolute light.

Your power of self-giving becomes supreme, universal.

Breathe out the magical perfume of the white rose to every member of humanity. Your in-breath receives and your out-breath gives.

As you give of your deepest and eternal self, you see the seeds of peace catching fire in the hearts of many receptive human souls across the earth, which interpenetrates even these exalted spheres.

You observe that the cherished seeds of peace are active, pregnant with myriad possibilities; and you understand that peace is a dynamic, ever-unfolding state of consciousness which will bear humanity on in the power of its free-handed giving to an inconceivably glorious destiny, individually expressed, omnipotent in its unity.

The Chinese sage gently draws the peace-giving ceremony to a close, although you are aware that within you its force lives on, and can always be given forth.

He leads you to an antechamber, which is like another temple, unbounded in its structure. You can see gardens and magnificent wildernesses, neither austere nor hostile, but hallowed and vigorous, which wind in and out of one another and are part of one another, mountainscapes and oceans, and a huge city glimmering softly with jewels in the far, far distance, hung with thin drifting mist-veils of blue and bridal-white.

You wonder what this place can be. The sage hears your unspoken question and says gently, 'My child, it your own spirit-home, your own temple. You have built this world within the inner scapes of your own heart, for therein lies the creative force.

'When you use your creative force to build, which is to give of the deepest essence of yourself, you add to your celestial temple.' He smiles and plucks as if from the air an immaculate golden flower, like a star and a lily, perfectly arrayed within as the petals of a yellow rose.

'Learn the Secret of the Golden Flower,' he says to you as he places the exquisite bloom in your hands. 'Within, you contain a holy and most magical power, which you must learn to seek with a pure heart; then you must learn to wield this power so that you may build, in the light of truth, a translucent life and a translucent earth − a life and a world which does not block and refuse the light, but allows it to express the brilliance of love.'

The ancient sage seems so beautiful in the soft light of the temple that you wonder if the Feng Bird is the bird-shape of the flame of his spirit. Again, he catches your thought and looks up through the domed glass roof of the temple, where the two birds, the Feng and your own spirit-bird, are still blithely wheeling.

'I will show you to whom the Feng belongs,' he says, smiling mysteriously.

You re-enter the Temple of Peace and walk into its gardens, which open around you like an embodied joy.

The Chinese sage leads you to a flowering peach-tree, and prepares to take his leave of you.

'Before we part,' he says, 'I will give to you a simple jewel of truth. Never overlook the power of the word. It is mighty. When you need to find peace in your earthly life, make of the word 'peace' a gentle, rhythmic chant. You will be enthralled by its mystical power, for it will be as if you summoned a great Angel of Peace to heal and renew you.'

The sage gives you his blessing. You exchange bows, and he returns to the shining temple. As he enters it, the domed building seems to become a measureless winged disc, radiant as the sun. When you look down at your hands to study the golden flower he put into them, you see that its image is now unmanifest, and you know that it has returned to your heart, from whence it came.

In the bird-fluting quietness, you hear the song of a swiftly running river. Within the music of its babble and laughter, you hear the sound of tearful, sobbing sighs.

Leaving the fragrant dell where the peach tree grows, you mount the grassy bank before you and pass into a shallow river-valley, where pastures of beautiful wild flowers, vivid and delicate, stretch to the river's edge.

The waters of the river are golden, of a pale celandine hue where they run past you, and of a deep and rich laburnum-yellow in the winding distance.

A group of rocks, glowing soft and clear like amber, grow out of the river's margin like a wild and scattered monument. Upon this outcrop a tall Chinese woman stands whilst the waters of the river lap her feet.

She is clothed in a high headdress surmounting traditional Chinese robes with flowing sleeves. Her figure is graceful and noble, and the radiant majesty of her face imparts to you that she is a goddess.

She holds a pitcher which she is pouring into the river. The pitcher is filled continually by her tears, which stream in crystal rivulets from her beautiful eyes.

Despite her queenly aura, you feel that the goddess is approachable. You walk to the outcrop of rock and ask her compassionately why she is so full of grief.

The goddess smiles through her flowing tears. 'Is not the sorrow of the earth cast up in us so that we may heal it?' she asks. 'If you have sometimes known sadness, but have not known its cause, you too have shared in this work.'

As she speaks, her tears cease and a light leaps up from

the golden river, casting rainbows through its spray as it surges over the rocks in its bed, and through the last of her tears as they are shed into the pitcher and poured into the body of the waters.

'I am Kuan Yin, Goddess of Compassion,' she says to you, 'and my pitcher contains the balm I pour forth on troubled waters. This is the Yellow River, the River of Life which flows forth into the physical world.

'How can it not bear sorrow on its breast? Yet that sorrow is the water which hollows a receiving chalice into the surface of the level stone. And the chalice is created so that it may be filled with joy. When the purpose of sorrow is understood, its distress can be soothed into peace.'

Kuan Yin steps down from her rock, leaving her pitcher at the water's edge. 'I shall return to it, by and by,' she says, 'but first you shall help me in another work.'

She takes your hand and leads you into an upward-sloping meadow where you can see the blissful gardens of the temple unfolding in beauty as far as your vision can reach.

'These are the Gardens of the Celestial Temple of the Sun,' she tells you. 'The Temple is the gateway to the Source, to the Everlasting Mystery which lies within the heart of the great central sun of your physical universe.

'These sanctified gardens belong to the Great Mother, Queen of Heaven, whom we call Si Wang Mu. Her holy spirit is everywhere! Under her divine authority, we shall perform a work of peace for your world.

'I am a goddess of compassion, but also goddess of mercy, goddess of prayers. As an act of divine mercy, I shall summon all the prayers for peace from earth's humanity which the Great Mother has received into her heart.'

As Kuan Yin falls silent, a tender breeze stirs and lifts your hair, spreading the robes of the goddess on the air currents and bearing with it the sweet incense of the gardens as an aromatic gift for your soul.

As if the fragrance sharpens your spiritual senses, you

hear a keening, beating sound from the west, and, looking that way, you see for a moment the dim twinkling shapes of mystic isles, far out on the western sea, caught in a violet haze upon the ocean's blue rim.

'Behold! They come!' says Kuan Yin, and there is song in her voice.

Suddenly you are surrounded by an endless flock of pure white doves. They mass and circle above you, giving forth their sweet purring cries.

They form the shape of an arrowhead and fly straight into the heart of the goddess. You are astonished to see that, within the space of an intake of breath, they have disappeared.

Kuan Yin smiles at your wonder, and opens her arms wide, as if in compassion, as if in embrace, to the earth-world which spins in darkness and sorrow within the world of the garden, although somehow far below and beyond it.

'Help me to send these birds of peace out into your world, as messengers from the Celestial Temple of the Sun,' she says to you.

Commanding the birds from your heart-centre, speeding them on wings of light to their sacred destination, you aid Kuan Yin as the whirring flock of doves are released from her heart in the perfect formation of the white rose of peace. They fly far, far away; but as you watch you see them settle all over the world in benediction, like atoms of the Angel of Peace. They seem to fill the face of the earth.

'Each one is a prayer offered for peace,' says Kuan Yin in her musical voice.

As you turn to look at her, you see that a few of the doves have not yet started on their journey, but are flying around both of you. As they swoop and flutter, the rays of the sun catch their plumage so that they shoot stars of white light out into the air.

Simultaneously they cast a shadow, so that shadow-birds also wheel around you.

Kuan Yin laughs in joy, and says to you, 'In my earthly country, we have a saying: "you cannot stop the birds of sorrow from flying through your hair, but you need not let them nest there."'

You watch entranced as birds of sorrow, birds of joy, fly around and around your head, now shadows, now glancing light. At last they too fly to earth to become birds of peace.

'Our work is nearly done,' Kuan Yin says. As she speaks, the golden Feng Bird and your own little spirit-bird fly overhead. They make straight for the heart of the sun, and disappear into its incandescent disc.

'Have no fear,' says the goddess. 'Your spirit-bird will return to you, as my bird, the Feng, will assuredly return to me.'

As you look at Kuan Yin, you see that her traditional robes echo the style, grace and fluidic beauty of the fiery Feng Bird, and you understand the significance of this, and of the Feng Bird which is the divine emblem of Kuan Yin and the Queen of Heaven...

Kuan Yin again takes you by the hand, and you descend through the inner spheres until you are back in your place of meditation once more. Before she leaves you she shows you a dove nestling at your heart-centre.

'Remember that the Doves of Peace will descend on your soul at your command,' she tells you; and then in parting she throws the brilliance of her love and protection around you as you end your meditation.

Return to normal consciousness, seal your centres (crown, brow, throat, heart and solar plexus) with the bright silver cross in a circle of light, and earth or ground yourself if necessary.

—⌒   A N G E L I C   S E E D · T H O U G H T   ⌒—

Close your eyes and you will see clearly.

Cease to listen and you will hear Truth.

Be silent and your heart will sing.

Seek no contacts and you will find union.

Be still and you will move forward
on the tide of the spirit.

Be gentle and you will need no strength.

Be patient and you will achieve all things.

Be humble and you will remain entire.

Taoist Meditation

Having contemplated the secrets of the heart, and become acquainted with the glorious bird of the soul, we can move on to a conscious meeting and attunement with the guardian angel.

You may like to make an altar before which you meditate, communicate, and pray to and with your guardian angel. This is by no means necessary, but it does sanctify a certain corner of your home, so that both the beautiful magnetic and radiant energies that you and your angels create together may not be disturbed or depleted. During the time that it is not in use, drape a piece of white cloth over your altar to protect it (I favour a white lace tablecloth, because the intricate patterns in the lace bring intimations to me of how angelic consciousness permeates and impregnates form with a delicate wonder and beauty that is endlessly creative and innovative).

Creating an Angel Altar

- Cover your altar with a white cloth (as its base).

- Place upon it a white and a gold candle, and a candle corresponding to the colour or colours of your guardian angel.

- Choose some treasured items from nature for your altar (a feather, a curiously-marked stone, a pearly snail-shell, dried rosebuds or rose petals, a piece of wood with a distinct form, fruit from the horse chestnut, etc.)

- A favourite aromatic oil in a burner will provide incense.

- Fragrant dried herbs can also be set on the altar to evoke the spirit of nature.

- Place some crystals near the candles in a clear glass bowl filled with water. You will find that the beauty of crystals becomes exquisite under clear water.

- Give space on your altar to a photo of someone who helps you to connect with your angels, perhaps someone you know intimately, or someone you admire.

- If you have one, place a cherished item from childhood on your altar.

- Choose a mandala that you find compelling, and apply your favourite colours. Put it in a photo-frame, and stand it up at the outer edge of your altar.

- Select a beautiful poem or an uplifting message, copy it by hand, and let it lie on the altar cloth.

- Find an image for your altar of some celestial or mythical being to whom you feel a soul kinship.

- An item of silver, and of gold, will help the balance of correspondences.

- A print of a painting or drawing by a favourite artist will play its part in refining the energies and atmosphere that flow around your altar-space.

- Make your altar beautiful, if you wish, with fresh flowers and scatterings of pearls, rosebuds and rose petals, clear quartz and rose quartz crystals (to represent the star and the rose in the heart).

Of course, there is no need to use as many items as are listed. Just a few objects of beauty may please you best. You do not need an altar to meditate, pray and commune with your angel. This can be done at any time, anywhere. But the angels have revealed that if we wish to heal with our guardian and other angels, we do need to arrange an altar so that the angels may establish a focal point for their concentrated and guided emanations. This will be discussed in a later chapter.

Meditation – Meeting Your Guardian Angel

Focus on your heart-centre and concentrate on your breathing for a few moments, quietly inhaling and exhaling 'through the heart'. Ensure that your spine is straight, relaxed and comfortable, supported if necessary. Through the simple rhythm of your breath, find the point of peace within, where all is calm and tranquil.

Go into the temple of the rose, so that you are surrounded by a gentle glow of colour like the heavenly rose hue in the first flush of the sky at sunrise. Feel the soft fragrant interior of this rose temple, delightful as silk and velvet to the touch, cool and yielding yet instinct with an enfolding intrinsic warmth. It is lit with the golden light of the radiant stamens at its centre; it is the essence of matter pure and perfected.

Move into the very heart of the rose.

Here is a golden arched door, carved with ancient and beautiful inscriptions which move and shimmer like living tongues of flame; for these holy words and symbols are eternally being spoken, forever in the act of becoming.

This is the magical door which leads through to the world of the angels. You may have caught glimpses of it in your dreams, or heard rumours of it in beautiful music and poetry.

Put forward your hands, and place them on the sacred door.

Your hands are loved by the angels, because they are instruments of blessing, healing and service. In the light of this profound understanding, feel the magic of the symbol of your hands and push open the door...

Step through...

You are in the world of the angels. Taste the pure air, the fragrance of the spiritual winds. Breathe in the celestial light, which plays in subtle rainbow colours around you and falls in laughing pools of silver and golden brightness around your feet. Walk over this perfect ground. All around you are the lovely forms of nature in their most radiant and exquisite expression.

Before you lies a pool, like a dream of peace. Kneel beside its still waters, tranquil as a perfect jewel, a crystal mirror.

Summer blue skies and the golden sun are reflected in the pool, as well as your own face. You are beautiful in the serene reflection of this liquid mirror.

Now a being of wondrous beauty takes form behind you, its great wings outspread in benediction and protection. You can see its reflected image in the pool: the sweetness of its face, the smile of peace on its lips, the kindliness in its eyes...

A swirl of colour, gentle in tone and pulsating with light, falls like a beautiful mystery over the surface of the pool and makes a dancing glory on the water...

What is the colour? Is there more than one?

Lock these secrets away in your heart.

Turn and face your radiant angel. It looks at you with eyes of ineffable, boundless love. With this love, in this love, it greets you.

Return its greeting.

The angel imparts to you that it is your guardian angel. No closer, more perfect, more reassuring friendship than yours with this being can exist.

Your guardian angel takes your hand and leads you to a seat nearby, made of pearl, which looks onto a paradise garden. Rest in the heavenly peace of this garden.

Your seat of pearl is the throne of your soul, and you are surrounded by happiness and wonder, safe in the loving embrace of your guardian angel's glorious aura.

Converse with your angel if you so wish. You will receive the answer to your questions in the stillness of your heart.

(Take time to enter deeply into meditation.)

You notice a great bright star, perfect in shape, hanging over the garden like a mystic lantern, blazing with a pure white light unlike anything seen on or from the earth.

With its mighty wings, like those of a mythical swan, your guardian angel lifts you right into the heart of the star, into its perfect radiance.

Listen, listen to the music of the spheres which surrounds you. Look into your heart.

Your angel has given you a precious gift. What is it?

Now you are floating, floating like a feather, floating in peace and happiness like a feather on the breath of God. Float down into your body, back into the room it inhabits.

Know that your guardian angel is always with you, and will take you again through the golden arched door into the world of the angels, to seek new horizons, deeper adventures of the soul, whenever you seek to go there in meditation.

Return to normal consciousness, seal your centres (crown, brow, throat, heart and solar plexus) with the bright silver cross in a circle of light, and earth or ground yourself if necessary.

—❀ A N G E L I C   S E E D · T H O U G H T S   ❀—

The wind is invisible; we only see its effect on
external forms, and it is in external forms that we
can see the divine spirit, the wind of God. Dissolve
your body in vision and pass into sight, pass into
sight, into sight!

Rumi (from Masnavi VI: 1459-60; 1463)

Oh, I swear by the afterglow of sunset,
And by the night and all that it enshroudeth,
And by the moon when she is at the full,
That ye shall journey on from plane to plane.

The Koran

Keeping an Angel Diary

Now that you have experienced a deep and intimate attunement
with your guardian angel, it is a good idea to begin to keep a diary to
record all your angelic encounters. A very vivid, beautiful, and
perhaps astonishing picture will start to emerge – a picture you may
not delineate in all its marvellous entirety if you keep no record of
events as they happen. Choose a diary bearing your angel's colour on
its cover, and use it only to record angel-related experiences.

Angelic Signatures

There are many ways of knowing that an angel has passed close by, or has touched your life and your heart with its wings of healing

- Just at, almost beyond, the outer edge of hearing, you may be aware of angelic whispers. These are not alarming or sinister in any way. On the contrary, you feel you want to hear them, and strain after doing so!

- A single white feather, drifting into your path, is a classic angel signature.

- Clouds often form themselves into magical and intriguing shapes – sometimes of fabulous creatures from myth and fairy tale – when the angels want to catch your attention. They also use clouds to form symbols and emblems, or your totem animal (the totem animal is the animal whose qualities and nature are a mirror of the elements that comprise part of your particular soul-identity).

- Birdsong has an angelic dimension. When it sounds very clearly and distinctly, becoming vibrant and enriched, stop what you are doing, and take the time to listen. The angels are speaking to you. Sometimes you will receive their message in words, in poetry and song. Sometimes, you just know, quite naturally, what they are saying. At other times, a quietness and stillness steals into the heart, wordless, hushed and profound; or you feel surrounded by peace and joy. This is truly an angelic gift.

- The behaviour of animals, wild or domestic, can indicate the presence of angels, and bring intimations of a message they wish to convey (for instance, on dark days, a pet animal might do something to cheer you or make you laugh).

- Strains of music, too subtle and delicate to be heard by the bodily ear, will play wondrous, remote harmonies to the inner ear. They denote the nearness of angels.

- Scents that stir the heart to wonder: of things too beautiful to be given earthly elucidation, unexplained flower fragrances, or as of rich aromatic woods and spices, signal the presence of angels.

- Playing, glancing colours of every delicate hue, some of them not of this earth and as though a gift from another world, announce that angels seek friendship and communion with you.

- Angels come to us so often in our dreams; but we fail to note down such dream encounters on first waking, and so miss many wonderful messages and sweet otherworldly intimations, that would otherwise be our companions throughout the earthly hours. It is sad that so many of these bright angelic gifts fall into the great gulf between our waking and our dreaming selves.

- The descent of a sudden stillness, like summer rain that falls soundlessly, yet hushes other sounds, reveals that angels are near. Breathe in this sacred stillness. It is their gift to our restless, suffering hearts.

- Echoes, subtle, faint and bell-like, of sweet laughter that surprise you and make you smile wonderingly, as if you believe it is your 'imagination' (the imagination is not a deceiver, as our modern world would have it to be) and yet truly know that it is not, signal that angels beckon to you from the radiant edge of perception, ready to give your soul wings of mystical fire.

- Unexpected intuitive knowledge of your heart, expressed in kindliness by a friend, is a sign that angels have given a message that has been received and understood, and passed onto you as an act of friendship, both human and divine. Coincidences, the sudden appearance of natural objects in your path (a floating leaf, a curiously-marked pebble, etc.), and even signs given through books and the media, are other ways that angels employ to speak to our hearts.

Keep alert, and note such things in your diary. However slight and subtle they may appear to be at the time, they will trace a miraculous design which will begin to reveal itself to you – a scrollwork whose intricate arabesques will catch the eye of your soul.

⟆ ANGELIC SEED-THOUGHT ⟆

THE GENTLE STARS

Sleep quietly, now that
the gates of the day are
closed. Leave tomorrow's
problems for tomorrow.
The earth is peaceful.
Only the stars are abroad;
and they will not
cause you any trouble.

Max Ehrmann

CHAPTER FIVE

THE BROTHERHOOD
OF ANGELS AND
HUMANITY

In the early years of the twentieth century, Geoffrey Hodson, the famous angel seer, began to receive very definite, even urgent, messages from the angels, concerning the approaching brotherhood of angels and humanity. The angels told him that there had been past ages where 'angels had walked with men', ages whose history we would marvel at today, as if we saw figures from myth and dream springing to life. Not only was such enchantment to revisit the earth in the future, but its principle, that of the brotherhood of angels and humanity, was to be applied in such measure as the earth and her peoples had never seen before. Having seemingly lost everything pertaining to our spiritual vision in long dark ages of heavy, earthbound materialism, humanity was to be restored to its true visionary status in unprecedented measure.

This was an astonishing promise, yet the angels insisted on its veracity. Apart from the considerable faith naturally accorded to the sincerity of such a genuine and gifted seer as Geoffrey Hodson, we are in any case beginning to see the establishment of that promised brotherhood today. More marvellous by far than the current fascination with angels, however, with all its books, recordings, workshops, talks and artwork (however helpful), will be the time when, again, we actually walk with angels, learning directly from them what, at present, our intuition and circumscribed inner vision can only whisper and hint at.

Whilst contemplating these things, I was strongly guided by an angelic source to compose a letter from the angels to humanity, attuning myself to the messages that Geoffrey Hodson had received, and yet also hearing those messages anew, expanded in line with the new consciousness we are offering the angels today. The letter is given below. Please read it as if it is personally addressed to you. This is the nature of the contact the angels would make with us – immediate, intimate and true – striking spiritual sparks of impact that will set ablaze our finer senses, and tear down the veil that we have thickly woven, of our own volition, between their domicile and ours.

It is in particular our guardian angel who will facilitate this process; and all guardian angels, under the rulership of Sandalphon and Michael, are called to action, to wait on their human charges for any sign that they are ready to receive this baptism of light into the angelic kingdom. All across the globe, our guardian angels are waiting to bear us into this new world at full flight, holding nothing back from those who are willing to prepare themselves. The call has gone out, and is heeded throughout the sphere of the guardian angels. Therefore, we might think of the angelic voice in the letter as proceeding particularly from our guardian angel, as well as from the angelic hosts. As you will see, the letter directly requests that we sign up to the brotherhood of angels and humanity.

Dear Child of Earth,

We greet you in love. We come to bring you joyful tidings of the new dawn of the Brotherhood of Angels and of Humanity.

We, the Angels, ask from you not worship – for that would be inappropriate – but love; asking only to be allowed to join with you in communion and thanksgiving to the Great Spirit who is Mother and Father of us all, and in adoration of the Supreme Teacher of Angels and of Humankind – the Spirit and the Bride.

The power of our prayers will be enhanced by being offered up with yours; your lives will be enriched by the answer to our common act of communion. Our sphere of usefulness to Divine Spirit will be enlarged by sharing yours; your lives will be enriched, your world made glad, by the inauguration of the Brotherhood of Angels and of Humanity.

The aim of the Brotherhood is to widen the range of human love by including the angels within its warm heart-light, so that the concept of brotherhood, the keynote of the coming age, shall know no bounds, but widen to include all living things, mortal and immortal – the dwellers in the ethereal worlds of air, fire, earth and water – the people of the limitless dominions of Space.

The time approaches when they will no longer remain invisible to you, for as you throw open your worlds to them, so will they cease to resist your entry into theirs; throwing wide their doors they will invite you to pass the portal, offering you full share of those treasures of incalculable value which they have guarded so long.

It is love that will open the doors; *love between yourselves first, so that you can never misuse the gifts they will bestow; love also for them, your brethren, to whom your love will give the power to reveal themselves.*

If only you knew what unlimited joy it brings us, the Angels, to give to you and to serve you, and what all-encompassing joy can come to you by calling on us continually in your endeavours, your high aspirations and your daily life. We pray that you may come to know, and that you will remember always that the handle of the door is on your side...

We, the Angels, send our love and our greeting to you, holding out our hands in fellowship, as bidden by the Lord, the Golden One, Who recently has come again to you and them. Surrounded by Angels, as of old, He-She comes, and we, His-Her servants, bear His-Her message of brotherhood and love – 'Be of the same mind, one with another, for there is but one Life, bound-

*less and inexhaustible, which is the very essence of you
all. Go to the children of Earth, draw close to them once
more, that those days may be brought back again when
Angels walked with humankind. Do this, it is the Will
of Divine Spirit'*

*Having this loving command laid upon us we come
to you, to bless you and to open the ears of your heart to
our message, offering you our service and our love, that
Divine Will be done.*

What will your answer be, Child of Earth?

We are advised that the coming age, whose birth we are attending,
will be particularly associated with the archangel Michael. Michael,
lord of all angels, is feminine as well as masculine. As his masculine
aspect is linked with the angelic aspect of the masculine Christ , so
is his feminine half connected with Brigid, the Bride; the feminine
Christ (the Spirit and the Bride). Because of wholesale denial of
the Sacred Feminine, Michael's feminine side has been obscured
and neglected. We need to understand Michael anew from this perspective, and discover his hidden feminine side.

Because Michael is an archangel of supreme significance, and
has charge over our guardian angels, it is important that we correct
our perceptions of him. The following guided visualization is
designed to help this process. You will find the hidden aspect of
Michael, his feminine counterpart, manifesting as the 'valley spirit',
the 'mysterious female' of whom Lao Tzu spoke so intriguingly.

Meditation – The Garden of Delights

Sit comfortably, spine upright, supported if necessary,
and breathe quietly and easily, a little deeper than usual.

Begin to imagine that you are walking peacefully upon a
high plateau. The wind blows softly through the whispering grasses and playfully stirs your hair. You look out on
the beautiful, wild mountainous region all around, gazing

quietly at the dreaming blue haze of the distant prospects.

You have come here to be at peace and to allow your soul to run free.

There is a hush over the land, made deeper by the sweet warbling song of a lonely mountain bird. Evening is drawing near, and the sunlight has taken on a rich, mellow valedictory brightness. Soon a pale green, amethyst and mystic blue luminous dusk gathers, creating a fairy world of muted light shining in the bosom of the clouds floating above the shadowed peaks.

In that magical twilight, shining bright trails of stars appear and dance with a gentle silver fire, as if some smiling hallowed spirit were offering a welcoming hand to your human soul, bidding it follow that mystical trail and ascend to dimensions of mystery and wonder where the heart laughs in bliss.

Contemplating these things, your soul rises within you and scintillates in a flame of joy, giving thanks for the magic of the evening.

In this heightened state, where hordes of shining eyes seem to keep on opening within you, you suddenly see what appears to be a wall. It stretches on and on across the land and into space. It is all around you, not imprisoning you or barring your way, but rather hiding, protecting, secreting, obscuring what lies beyond.

As you gaze at the wall, so impregnable and yet misty, glimmering and ever-changing like the imponderable stars, a miracle happens. A great angel, golden and glorious as the rising sun, takes form before your eyes. It spans the horizon, and the ethereal wall begins and ends within its aureole of perfect golden light.

An interior voice says: 'Behold Archangel Michael,' and with awe and reverence you bathe in the radiance of this magnificent being.

As you absorb his brilliant light, your own wings take shape and spread behind you. Though you remain standing where you are, you feel your soul take flight and soar into the heaven worlds.

The archangel Michael opens his arms to receive you, and you realize that his form has become that of a gateway, mighty, arched and pillared. It is open to you.

Wondering, you walk forward as into the rays of a dazzling star.

There is a garden here beyond the walls. And yet, when you turn to look back, there are no walls; they have dissolved away into the gentle sunshine, and everywhere there are the playing golden rays of Michael, of the sun, and of some ineffable mystery of Being above these.

You turn again to the garden, eager to explore. This is the Garden of Delights, and everywhere you look there are wonders.

You see that not only are the golden rays playing all over the garden, but that the most delicate rainbow colours are everywhere present like subtle laughing flames... and there are other colours too, colours you have never seen on earth, which speak to and sound notes within your soul so that it emanates a strange and lovely music.

Stand awhile and bathe in these glorious, rejoicing colours as they caress you with their heart-awakening voices.

Your feet sink into sun-warmed grass, emerald and cool in its depths. These lawns are starred with tiny, jewel-coloured flowers which cluster around your toes. They call to you with bell-like voices to follow the path they make.

You set your feet on the path, and as you take your first steps, you can hear every vibrant grass blade whispering songs of praise into the gently sighing wind, which does not blow but lightly breathes, revivifying your own breath.

You walk across the glowing green lawns to where a rose garden is laid out in a sacred spiral along curving paths of clear crystal. Each rosebush reaches almost to your own height, and is burgeoning with a glorious pageant of roses, as if they spilled from the heart of an angel. Foaming billows of lush rose-heads surge and flow on each side, springing into the air in a burst of colour and an ecstasy of perfume so that your senses have to expand and grow to encompass their reality.

Walk amongst the roses to the very centre of the spiral.

There, amongst the tumbling, intoxicating roses, stands a white boulder.

It speaks to you, and its voice is like bee-song, vibrating on many levels.

'Come to the centre, child of earth. Take the path to your heart.'

You feel a surge of love for this being of stone and you pass into what seems to be its arms. You enter a moment of blazing white light. Beyond it stretches another garden, although you know that it is simply a deeper dimension of the same garden.

This garden is like the last, only wilder, sweeter airs blow about it. Within its precincts there are little sunlit woods, a clear tranquil lake, and wild turf crowded with tiny, star-like flowers of a thousand vivid carnival hues which rolls away like a gentle wave, creating miniature hills and dells and hollows in its swell.

You stand awhile to watch and listen as birds and beasts of great beauty come and go, without timidity or aggression. They are a part of the peace, givers and receivers of the Divine Love which breathes everywhere as a holy radiance, a holy fragrance, a mysterious omnipotence. It dances upon the waters of the lake on the wind so that its ripples shake and laugh with joy.

As you listen, you become aware that the trees are singing hymns of great and ancient beauty. You are drawn into their music, absorbing their might, their grandeur, their nobility of spirit.

Above you in the vast, deep-hearted ocean of cerulean

blue sky, shining white clouds build mystic temples of blissful purity.

'Human soul, hear what we say! The time will come when these temples that we are showing you will appear every-where on your earth! And when those days are with you, humankind shall know that all the earth is a Most Holy Temple!'

You realize that the clouds have spoken to you; and in wonder you contemplate that in the Garden of Delights, the stones speak, the trees sing, the clouds prophesy and the water and the winds dance and laugh. All share in a sublime consciousness which magically dwells at the centre of your heart.

Recognizing this great truth, your spirits become even more light and airy, and you are filled with a childlike joy.

In this new innocence, you climb the little, flower-strewn hill which lies before you.

You are soon at the top, and you look down on a sight which is the essence of paradise.

Here, spreading before you, is a precious and sacred valley. It gives you its name. It is the Many-Coloured Valley, and it is a dale of abundant supernaturally beauti-ful summer flowers, each radiating its own exquisite hue as if lit by an inner, angel-bright luminescence.

Springs rise everywhere, making natural fountains of crystal purity. Its perfume and its rapturous colours, its 10,000 jubilant flower-forms, fill you with an ecstasy of beauty and mystery. As a child you run down into the valley, feeling the welcoming caress of the soft, heavenly-scented petals as if some divine soul of motherhood waited there to receive you.

And now you feel the Holy Presence of someone, some Being of inconceivable magnitude, in the heart of which you live and move and have your being.

It is one Being, and yet two. It is the Lady and the Lord of the Garden. As your consciousness is raised so that you may achieve a humble realization of this Being, its two aspects merge into one.

You understand at last that it is the Beloved!

You kneel at the feet of this Great Spirit, this inscrutable Presence, and you are filled with a deep, deep peace. Heavenly peace fills the craters of your need. Your body melts away in peace. Your heart rests in the vast ocean of peace which is the Heart of the Beloved. Your mind is released from its restless tides and becomes as serene as a soundless, motionless lake, reflecting the sublime peace of the Beloved. Your emotional self becomes a white dove of peace. Your soul is transfigured into a shining angel of peace by the healing balm that is the breath of the Beloved.

All is peace, and the Beloved is All.

You are aware that the Beloved has transported you to a spiritual mountaintop. And yet, magically, miraculously, you are still in the arms of the valley of flowers. You are free upon the glorious mountaintop, and simultaneously cradled within the sacred valley.

All the flowers of the valley merge into the form a single rose upon the radiant mountaintop. The rose is aflame with the light of the Beloved.

In peace you enter its heart, its temple. Step within, and know that the Lord of the Garden and the Valley Spirit will guide you safely home, and dwell within you always.

Touch down gently, become aware of the familiar things around you, and seal your centres.

Rudolf Steiner, the esoteric philosopher and teacher, describes how, in earlier ages, men and women could meet Archangel Michael as in a kind of lucid dream, but 'since the end of the last third of the nineteenth century, men [members of humanity] can meet Michael in the Spirit, in a *fully conscious way*'.

Michael and his feminine essence are imparting a very special teaching and a very beautiful service to present-day humanity. They are not only inspiring us to purer and greater expressions of the divine light that dwells within us, but they are endowing our heart-directed earthly deeds with a radiant substance of angelic gold that, as Rudolf Steiner says, 'carries the earthly deed out into the cosmos; so that it becomes cosmic deed'. In other words, our light-orientated efforts are being freed from their earthly limitations and are taking on the nature of godly acts, thanks to the blessing of Michael and his feminine counterpart (whom I believe is correctly conceptualized as an aspect of, or a sister to, Brigid, the feminine essence of Christ, as in truth, Michael is an aspect of, or angelic brother to, the male aspect of Christ).

This is a truly wonderful scenario! It means that, when we work for the light, attuned to the Christ, to our higher mind, and to the angels, our deeds are divinely amplified and magnified beyond imagination! If only we keep steadfastly on our path, giving of our light-selves, we need have no fear for our polluted planet, for the strangulation of its eco-systems, or for any of the monumental and multitudinous problems facing humanity and its animal brethren today. All will be healed, all brought into balance, harmony and peace, if only we will faithfully 'keep on keeping on'. What a birthright and a stupendous future is ours, if we will only claim it! And what a sense of upliftment and encouragement we should take from the knowledge of this miraculous gift of Michael!

There is a fairy tale of a simple, humble girl in straitened circumstances who descended into the Well at the World's End and performed kindly and helpful deeds within the magical realm that she found there, and then passed out of the Well again through a shower of supernatural gold, which remained with her so that she returned as a being of light who could work miracles throughout the rest of her life in the everyday world. Thus our deeds will become miraculous through the golden touch of Michael. It is our promise and our destiny, when we heed Michael's call to reach up into our heavenly or angelic selves, and act from that point, the selfsame point which is to be found deep in the heart.

Michael's gift cannot come to us without the devotion and co-operation of our own guardian angel. The guardian angel it is who wakes us gently, as with caresses, to the sense of our greater destiny; for the guardian angel has charge, not only over our personal day-to-day life, but of our individual part in the great plan that was laid down for every member of humanity before the physical cosmos came into being.

Within this great scheme the guardian angel does not work alone. Not only Michael, but also the great angel who has Earth in his-her care, Sandalphon, influences the guardian angel; for Sandalphon has supreme charge over guardian angels. Yet the overlighting angel whom our guardian works with most intricately of all is our zodiacal angel; for in the mystery of the constellation of stars under whose influences we were born into our present incarnation lies the pattern, the plan, and the deeper meaning of our lives.

So the guardian angel is linked with the great planetary angels who act under the command of the Lords of Karma, and who through astrological processes overlight the karmic path through life of each individual human being according to their sun sign. When a soul is ready to incarnate, alignment of the exact planetary forces is necessary to ensure that the incoming soul is born into the precise circumstances it needs to continue to make its own unique progress towards spiritual realization. There is one angel above all others who is with us from before our conception until after our earthly 'death'. This is the famous guardian angel; and every member of the human family is allotted one of these angelic companions, without fail, no matter what the circumstances, each time he or she incarnates upon the earth.

The guardian angel, under the command of a hierarchy including the planetary angel or angels to whom it is connected, is instrumental in bringing the prospective parents together and helping to build the body of the incarnating soul, complete with all its subtler vehicles, within the womb. The planetary beings with whom the guardian angels work to fulfil this task build each embryonic human body upon the same principles used to build the cosmos, and implant within it the same creative dynamism with which the universe is instinct. Thus, each human being is a microcosm of the macrocosm. Humanity is created in the image of the Godhead.

The planetary angels of our solar system are associated with, or are projections of, the 'Seven who stand around the Throne', the seat of consciousness of Divine Spirit. Seven is the sacred number of creation, and the first seven planets that exist in our solar system comprise the physical or lowest spiral of this mystic number. The remaining planets begin the scale again as higher harmonics of the seven lower planets; and then the issuing essence of the number seven continues on and on to the highest heights beyond our conception, wherefrom the seven great rays of creation initiate into being all that lives and moves and is possessed of consciousness. At the head of each of these rays stands a member of the Elohim, the Great Ones who create a formation around the Throne of Goddess-God. The names of the planetary archangels are:

Michael, ruler of the sun, on whom we should call for strength, spiritual protection, revelation, truth and enlightenment; his day is Sunday.

Raphael, archangel of Mercury, on whom we should call for healing, energy, knowledge, cleansing and self-mastery; his day is Wednesday.

Anael or **Haniel**, archangel of Venus, on whom we should call for love, compassion, harmony, beauty and wisdom; this great archangel of Venus is also closely associated with the Earth Angel; her day is Friday.

Gabriel, archangel of the moon; on whom we should call for assistance with our hopes, dreams, aspirations and the birth of new projects and all things to do with motherhood, physical birth, babies and children, and those aspects of spirituality which are associated with Divine Mother, and for strength to overcome fear; her day is Monday.

Samael or **Camael**, archangel of Mars, on whom we should
call for courage, empowerment, protection of the
innocent, willpower, stimulative energy; his day is
Tuesday.

Sachiel or **Zadkiel**, archangel of Jupiter, on whom we
should call for the upholding of justice, law and order,
wisdom, humour, beneficence, abundance, success,
generosity.

Cassiel, archangel of Saturn, on whom we should call for
peace, harmony, serenity and in all those situations in
life when we need the grave wisdom of the recording
angels (to do with past and present lives, the Akashic
record, the history of humanity and the earth, etc.).

Here are some words from the ascended teacher White Eagle on
the angels of the planets, who 'flock' or 'harmonize' under their own
archangel, the guardian angel of each planet:

Interpenetrating all the earth life are the rays of the
planets... As we tread the path of evolution, so we strive to
understand and receive more fully into our being these
vibrations of life. When a soul has learnt to vibrate harmoniously with all forms of life, then it has attained
mastership.

We ask those of you who have not yet become conscious
of the power of the planetary influences over the earth, to
endeavour to realize their presence, their influence, and
the blessings which these angelic forces are pouring forth
upon humanity. The angel messengers from other planets
come to strengthen your higher bodies. They work with
you, enabling you to send forth, to other human beings,
strong and clear rays of light. No light is wasted, because it
is reflected and it will return to you and cause your higher
and subtler bodies to become pure and strong and recep-

tive and active upon the higher planes of your life.

The messengers, or angelic ones, from Mercury are becoming very active at the present time. The influence that comes from them is to help you attain self-mastery. In your daily life, if you will respond to these angelic ones, that self-mastery will direct you to attain perfection in action, in thought, in attunement to the cosmos.

The messengers who come to help humanity from the planet Venus bring harmony into your life, harmony into the centre of your being. These angels embrace and bring wisdom, for the angels of Venus are so lovely, they are all-love and beauty. Self-mastery, harmony and love – the wisdom and the love of the angels of Mercury and Venus – have the greatest power for the perfecting of the human race.

Then there are those silent recorders, the angels of Saturn, whom we would call the angels of the light. They will not let a soul pass onwards until it has learnt the exact and precise lesson which must be learnt. Angels of Saturn move slowly and surely, but they help humanity reap a goodly harvest, rich and golden. The angels from Saturn and Mercury are so brilliant.

The angels of Uranus sound the trumpet call; they come sweeping through, bringing a breaking-up of solid conditions which have been crystallized and set by Saturn. This cleansing and purification is an aspect of Father-Mother God perhaps not yet understood by the young in spirit.

If things are swept out of your life, know that all is constructive, all is good. Work in harmony with the forces of God, and see in everything construction, evolution, growth and beauty.

Then the work of the angels of Mars is of the utmost value to humankind, bringing stimulation, bringing increased light, bringing the courage and the energy which you all need to progress on the path.

The angels of Jupiter, who are now coming into closer

contact with the earth, stand with the scales and bring law and order, and through their influence a wonderful beneficent power is absorbed by those souls who are particularly attuned to the vibrations of Jupiter.

...It is impossible to deal adequately with these profound truths. We ourselves have only caught a glimpse of the grandeur of the universe: only a glimpse of the possibilities which lie within us all. But each time you endeavour to reach the high places of the heavenly light, you are making a contact with powerful angelic forces, for in each one of you is the magnetic attraction by which you are brought into tune with angelic power, with a planetary ray. These rays are experienced in different degrees, but in you, individually, lies the power to attract and absorb into your being your own particular planetary forces.

It is 'your own particular planetary forces' with which your personal guardian angel is linked, to help you absorb and respond to them throughout your span of earthly life. A guardian angel is steadfastly with each human soul during every moment it spends on earth, either sleeping or waking; and at its demise its guardian angel receives it into the spiritual worlds, working with the kindly Angel of Death to gently unbind it and lift it entirely away from the knotted cords of earth (if the soul will permit it) and standing surety for it on the other side of the veil.

The guardian angel cannot prevent its human charge from meeting his or her karma along the way, but it can protect against unnecessary pitfalls and accidents. It can help to steer a path through the soul's karma so that its effects are creative rather than destructive, and if the soul will really listen to and respond to the promptings of its angel, it is even possible to absolve or rise above the karmic stumbling-block so that its impact is negated. It is no exaggeration to say that if we would all attune constantly and sincerely to our guardian angels, humanity's experience of earthly life would be immeasurably changed.

Is a different guardian angel appointed to us each time we incarnate? Some say this is so, and it makes sense when we consider the different needs and conditions and planetary influences of each incarnation. Yet there are others who confidently claim that their guardian angels have been with them throughout countless lives, since both were born or breathed into a state of being from the heart of Goddess-God; and that although the guardian angel inhabits sacred rather than linear time, so that simultaneously it can foster the growth of others incarnate in distant galaxies as well as its human companion on earth, its connection with all its charges are sacred bonds wrought in divine forges and such bonds are never broken.

It is true that the angel and the human relationship exists to serve the physical and the spiritual universe and is never pulled off course to minister to purely personal or selfish fulfilment. Yet it may be, within the infinite mysteries of the divine and cosmic heart, that there is a point of balance where the angel and the human become one – not in any static or unalterable sense because we are assured by many teachers that humankind has its own spiritual path and was not created simply to be subsumed into the angelic – but for the purpose of forming a bridge between the physical and the spiritual spheres so that matter itself might be irradiated and redeemed.

The idea of human and angel combining the essence of their being to spiritualize dark matter in this way seems to have a potency, a music congruent with beauty and therefore with truth; and perhaps, in order to attain the harmonization necessary to create such a bridge, human and angel are permitted a personal and eternal bond, weaving it in such a manner as to overcome the restrictions and the exclusiveness of personal love (arising from the human source) without abandoning its peculiar poignancy and radiance (unawareness of which would arise from the angelic source). And it certainly must be true that, although the human and the angel remain two distinct aspects of the Divine, the evolving consciousness of both are so exquisitely intertwined and commingled that one cannot exist without the other. Perhaps this notion of a fused angelic and human bridge between heaven and earth is symbolized perfectly in the mystic span of the rainbow, and embodies yet another dimension of the mystery of human and angel lovers?

Whether or not the guardian angel and its human companion are together forever and are caught up in a shared destiny, it is safe to say (again) with certainty that your angel cannot assist you unless you are willing to accept its help. It cannot and would not override its human companion's free will, for although we use it to get ourselves into hot water most of the time, our free will is nevertheless a most precious and sacred gift, perhaps the greatest gift of all, because through it we will attain to individual God-realization – in a sense, to God status.

The angels – and particularly our guardian angels – are hampered in their work for us by our unawareness, our unconsciousness of the vital bonds that exist between them and ourselves. Where there is not even a faint glimmer of perception regarding them, their efforts are often stifled. And yet they need only the smallest acknowledgement, the shyest invitation, to come to our aid and eventually to flood our lives with light.

One common misconception to take into account when building your relationship with your guardian angel is that angels know all there is to be known. Angels can certainly draw on spiritual wisdom and knowledge direct from its source, and their consciousness is not circumscribed or limited as ours is. William Blake said of them, 'I have always found that angels have the vanity to speak of themselves as the only wise; this they do with a confident insolence sprouting from systematic reasoning.' Yet angelic messages convey that they have much to learn from us. Unsurprisingly, they are not wise in the ways of our world and they know little of the restlessness and inappeasability of the heaving emotional tides of human experience, even though they are attuned to our individual suffering and long to bring us comfort, healing and solace.

Therefore it is helpful to the guardian angel for us to express how we feel as we live our lives, to teach our companion, in a sense, how it is that our problems arise from our human relationships, from our hopes and our dreams, our aspirations and disappointments, our insecurities and fears.

Our angels are always delighted to make contact with us, unlike our human friends! We can write such information in a letter to our angel (see Chapter Two), or, when the environment allows, we can speak openly to our guardian. We do not need to analyse, just simply to connect with our feelings and describe them. From one perspective, our guardian angel is all-knowing. From another, it is an evolving and learning being, as we ourselves are. Perhaps it is that angels are outward bound, whilst we are homeward bound.

Whilst our guardian angel will gently prompt, guide, instruct, enlighten and awaken the human soul, it will also facilitate communion with other angels whom we may need to contact for their help, as well as with our loved ones beyond the veil, and especially with our guide, our helpers and our master (the teacher under whose spiritual guidance we are progressing, who is generally discarnate and who is as often female as male). There are also fairylike or elemental creatures who help us, and who are under the authority of our angel. Our human master, guide, loved ones and helpers are present to foster the evolution of our consciousness. Our angels are present to ensoul the qualities and virtues we need to inculcate within ourselves, and to build, perfect, beautify and spiritualize form on every level of existence.

Everything within our experience that is beautiful, joyful, inspiring, ennobling, imbued with wonder-inducing qualities or shot through with magnificence or an ineffable delicacy and tenderness of touch in its manifestation is brought to us by angels. Together, our exalted human teachers and our immeasurably bright angels create an ascending arc or a spiral stairway to heaven which calls our soul ever onward and upward.

As you strengthen and energize the bonds and points of connection between yourself and your guardian angel, you will not work in isolation, for the good of yourself alone. Any work associated with angels cannot be contained within such limitation, for, being in essence architects and builders, it is their nature to balance the benefit of the unit with the good of the whole. Whenever a human soul makes the effort to create a conscious link with its angels, especially its guardian angel who will work with a much greater skill and dedication to open and quicken the channel than its human counterpart can, the way is made clearer and easier for other humans and angels to draw closer to each other in conscious communion.

Our guardian angel can give us almost magical assistance with our human relationships and with our own journey into freedom and happiness if we will only call upon it to do so. We simply need to ask in order to receive. The gifts are abundant and precious, but it is important to ask for them in the right way. We might think of six steps as necessary to achieve this:

Make a lucid decision as to the virtue or quality that you need to receive. If you are unsure, ask your angel for clarification and write down its answer.

Let go of any negative or egotistical feelings pertaining to the situation. Ask for help to do this if necessary.

Enunciate your request clearly, using spoken words. Ask from your innermost heart, really opening yourself in humility and gratitude and joy to the gift that is to be given to you. This will help to eradicate any lurking subconscious resistance to it. If you ask casually or superficially, you fail to create the necessary receptacle within yourself which will contain your gift until it infuses into your nature.

Become aware of your guardian angel's enfolding presence. Receive your gift and give thanks. Send love to your angel.

Be alert to the array of little opportunities which will arise to practise your new-found quality or skill in your everyday life. These are given to you to marry the tendencies of your inner nature with your gift, and must be made use of.

Remember that when an angel's gift has to supplant a deep-rooted negativity in order to become established, it will be necessary to repeatedly renew the request for the gift, asking each day over a period of many days, weeks or perhaps even months. The gift is given faithfully each time, but cannot at first be retained by the recipient. Each ceremony of asking and receiving strengthens the recipient's soul until, at last, the gift is transformed into a

quality of that soul, inherent in its very structure. Persevere. Angels are everlastingly patient and eager to help us!

The gifts you might ask for are those of insight, patience, compassion, understanding, assertiveness, humour, forgiveness, generosity; protection and healing after abuse and the right way to resolve the destructive situation; wisdom, trust, joy, security, inner peace; the ability to promote harmony; the transformation of fear and anger into constructive action or decision and finally into peace; the way to take back your power and re-centre yourself if you have been pressurized into giving it away; firmness, resolution, clear-seeing, fairness and even-handedness...the list is endless. Feel the need or the lack in yourself, and fill it abundantly from your angel's store.

Whatever the skill or the quality you require, your guardian angel will call to your aid that quality's ensouling angel and will transmit its frequencies, its vibrational essence, to you.

Often your angel will suffuse you with a colour which will wash your gift into your soul. Perhaps you need wisdom. What colour is wisdom? It could be a ray of amethyst, for acceptance; or the blue of the heavens for release into tranquillity; or the eastern rose of sunrise to enable the heart to open. Such are the gifts of the angels, and they will never be withheld from you.

The guardian angel is endowed with a truly wonderful gift for healing our personal relationships. Here is a simple exercise which will gently open our subtle faculties to receive it in full measure.

In your imagination, go into a golden rose healing temple and sit with your angel, face to face.

Express all your pain, anxiety, disquiet, panic, irritation, or sense of injustice. Pour it all into your angel.

Listen to your angel's responses, which may not always come in words so much as in caressing waves that qualify feelings, like a gentle clarifying dew that steals on your darkness as the rays of the morning, bringing fresh perspectives and touching the viewpoints of your inner landscape with new-born, angelic radiance. You may

perceive that these brightening viewpoints are beaded with life-giving, starry droplets of abundant and loving possibility, giving you unexpected insights and delightful mirror-reflections of the beauty of your angel, which dwells in the heart of the rising sun.

From your chaotic, churning state of mind, your angel will lead you to a soft blue lake of peace and bathe you tenderly in its shallows.

Then it will take you further out, and allow you to immerse yourself in the water, through which you can breathe.

It will call angels of clarity, light and humour to you. It will surround you with angels of compassion — compassion given to you and your situation so that you, in your turn, are enabled to perceive compassionately — and angels of inner poise and power.

It will place a pearl-pink rose in your heart-centre.

Send the fragrance of that rose to the person or situation that distresses you.

Angels of Sorrow

Our guardian angel will surround us with these gentle, compassionate angel brethren, who will approach us with sweet tenderness and consolation, transforming our hard, dark, bitter and painful feelings into a nurturing flow of tears, which brings forth beauty, sweetness, and the gift of heart-deepening, from our sadness and distress. Our heart needs to be carved from an incontinent flat plane into a bowl that can be filled, a receptive chalice or vessel. This is sorrow's beautiful purpose, and the poignant benediction of the angels of sorrow. Don't be afraid of them, or offer any resistance. They are loving angels. Let them softly enfold you, and put the spirit of beauty like a flame into your heart.

Afterwards, bring in the angels of humour! The angels of sorrow and the angels of humour work in tandem, creating a perfect partnership. That is why so many of our great humorists are also men and women of sorrow, and why there is sometimes a feeling of euphoria at funerals! After sorrow, we laugh. Our balance is not only restored, but our experience of life is abundantly enriched.

This exquisite weft of the angels of sorrow and the angels of humour brings to mind the old Chinese adage: 'It may be inevitable that the birds of sorrow fly through your hair, but you can make sure that they don't nest there!'

Initiating Dialogue

If someone is troubling you because of their behaviour or attitude, or if you have concerns regarding a friend, a colleague, or a family member, you can initiate dialogue with their guardian angel. The process is simple:

Sit quietly, and go to your heart-centre, that sacred altar where we link with our guardian angel. If you are very upset or worried, use one of the exercises previously given for finding the point of stillness within; or just simply find the inner heart by seeing your emotions and your mind as heaving, aggressive, grey seas gently being transformed into a sweet, still, blue lagoon by the magical touch of your guardian angel. Then let the mind rest, supported and at peace, in the warm, loving, hushed ocean of life.

When you are at ease, ask your guardian angel to link you to the other person's guardian angel, and to their higher self.

Feel your guardian angel creating the link. It will be done under the auspices of your guardian by an angel of communion.

Speak through that angel of communion to the other person's guardian angel, and to their higher self. Speak encouraging, loving words, even though you are setting out plainly what worries or distresses you. The angels will not accept force, anger, abuse, manipulation, demands or nagging! Just speak lovingly and positively, recognizing

throughout that the other person is truly a brother or sister to your heart, whatever the situation.

Close by sending light to the other person, and to their guardian angel.

Whenever you commune with your guardian angel, or feel its presence throughout the day, send it your human love. This wave of love will always carry an essence of divine love. Your angel delights in receiving your love, and will joyfully respond with an answering wave of angelic love whose power of healing and blessing is a thousand fold of what it has received. Archangel Michael is at work here, blessing your deed through your guardian angel with miracles of magnitude and amplification.

Warrior Angels

Sometimes, if you are struggling with a problem which begins to take on the proportions of an unconquerable foe (jealousy, addiction, obsession or ungovernable rage, for instance) or you are in spiritual danger (perhaps someone is seeking to drain your will using forbidden psychic means) your guardian angel will send what are called warrior angels to assist you. We can call on these warriors at any time through prayer, but our guardian angel will always be instrumental in summoning them to our aid, as it is, so to speak, a link in the chain of command. The warrior angels are spoken of as wearing headdress and armour, and appear to our human conception as enormous in size and powerfully muscular.

Our struggle for self-mastery against spirits of the darkness is always helped and applauded by our guardian angel. When we can overcome and master fear, trusting instead in the goodness of the Great Spirit and secure in the knowledge that Goddess-God has us in its safekeeping and has set angels over us and under us to preserve us always, our guardian angel draws very close, surrounding us and feeding us with a fathomless love. When we pass such tests of the spirit, the whole earth is raised up and helped forwards on her journey into the light.

So many experiences tempt us to think of the human race and the earth in terms of darkness; but it is one of our great soul-lessons to always hold firmly to the truth that the darkness is only a cloak or shroud of illusion, and behind it blazes the one true light, inextinguishable and undiminishing. At the heart of all experience, the Light is waiting to gently encompass our mind and our heart.

When a situation arises that upsets you and stays with you, try the following technique:

Create a white rose with the wizardry of your imagination.

Place the person or the experience, and the vibrations within you created by that person and the situation, or the experience, within the heart of the rose.

See the rose enfold these vibrations and associations within itself. Its petals close over them.

Ask your guardian angel to dissolve the rose.

See the rose melt away, and completely disappear.

Of course, the role of our guardian angel is not only to heal and regenerate painful and blocked relationships. It is also very much part of its function to bless and to empathize with our joy in our loving, beautiful, sweetly-attuned relationships; so share these with your angel, too. Your harmonious relationships will become even lovelier, their sphere of benign influence wider, their intrinsic creative power quickened, if you bathe them in your angel's light.

If, during your more difficult times, you need a deeper connection with the Lake of Peace, to whose shores your angel will bear you when you need its healing, use the following meditation.

Meditation – The Lake of Peace

When the unsettling ripples of life's setbacks and disappointments threaten your peace of mind, or guilt and fear rise from the depths to haunt you, find solace in Vishnu's Lake of Perfect Peace, 'sanctified as the clear mind of a devotee'.

Sit upright, your spine supported if necessary, and ensure that you are comfortable and relaxed. Focus on your heart-centre and breathe gently, easily and slowly. In your mind's eye, let your heart be as a jewel or a crystal into which you are gazing.

You are standing beneath the boughs of a tree in a forest at the breaking of a summer dawn. A soft cascade of birdsong sounds in the still, cool air, a sweet liquid piping and fluting which seems to be from far, far above, as though it echoed in the grand, solemn space of a temple. The silver-grey light of the early morning has a rapt, enthralled quality, like a beating heart in a lover's expectant breast.

The rays of the rising sun smile suddenly over the waiting forest, and all is transformed. The birdsong becomes a mighty chorus of joy; you listen and watch in rapture as small woodland animals appear in the forest glade before you, intent upon the business of the morning. They are unafraid, showing only curiosity and friendliness as you turn your gaze on them.

With you, they are aware of the presence of Brahma or the Great Spirit and, with you, they offer thanksgiving for the birth of this perfect day.

You are wearing robes as if composed from the new-born sunlight and the viridian green of springtime leaves. You notice that there are translucent jewels sewn into your clothing which catch the light in dancing flashes and simultaneously give it forth again in shades of their own mystic brilliance.

On your feet are soft shoes made from cloth of gold. The threads in them shine in the sunbeams, and as you begin to walk deeper into the singing forest it is as if every step you take can heal and bless the earth with sacred gold from the heart of the sun.

You realize that you have been given these shoes to tread softly upon the Earth, to revere and worship her with an offering of your human love, for verily she is a loving, living Goddess, born from the heart of Divine Mother.

Every step you take is one of jubilance and wonder. You listen to the birdsong, you taste and smell the clean, fresh, vigorous scents of the woodland, you see the sunlight dancing on the leaves and the forest floor, and the sapphire vault of the skies rolling like a blue carpet of peace over all the world.

It occurs to you that all creation is dancing with the Goddess and that it would be good for you to dance too. You dance there in a shining glade among the trees, lightly, airily, like a spirit of nature, and it seems to you in your joy as if you danced with the scintillating daylight stars and all the turning firmament.

When you have danced to your heart's delight, you rest awhile and then press on deeper and deeper into the forest because you know that some marvel awaits you further on among the trees.

You approach an ancient and majestic tree whose great arching branches create a quiet green sanctuary blessed with fragrant ariel flowers. As you walk around its huge bole, you see that its mighty prehensile roots coil away with serpentine dignity to the shores of a beautiful lake, set like a serene jewel at the great open heart of the forest, its bright waters calm and clear under an enchantment of deepest peace.

You have come to the magical and legendary Lake of Peace.

With reverence, as though you walked on holy ground, you approach its verge, where reeds stand in contemplation of their graceful reflection in the limpid water. You rest upon the short mossy turf and look out over the lake.

The sun is shining, and the cerulean blue of the skies together with its few clouds, lit with a pure angelic-white radiance, are mirrored in perfect stillness in the fathomless depths.

As you gaze, you begin to notice that the reflections in the water are changing. The image of a wondrous mandala, a sacred pattern inside a revolving wheel, is taking shape within the lake. Its dimensions are those of your own soul. It is a pathfinder to the centre of all things, to the centre of the Great Spirit, the Heart of All, where you have your being and your dwelling and your true reality.

Enter the heart of the mandala reflected in the lake and rest there in deep peace. You can breathe with ease and delight in these soft, pure waters.

Now you know that the Lake of Peace is indeed the mirror of your eternal self.

You begin to see that on the further side of the lake the forest has become even more beautiful. All is as before, yet the blessing of the trees and the lake and the sunlit spaces has a greater profundity. The circle of the mandala completes itself, and you are in the heaven worlds. You have left the lake, for it lies ahead of you once more, a lake of yet deeper, heavenly peace.

You are in the enchanted forest of the spirit, and between the lofty trees, which are hung simultaneously with fruits and flowers and fabulous birds which sing with voices of gold and silver, you can see areas of pasturing grass aflame with flowers of every hue, vibrant with unearthly colours which scintillate like dancing lights.

Songbirds, like fiery jewels, and long-feathered birds of paradise dart and swoop overhead. From the south of the forest, the sweet bell-like notes of many cuckoos sound, and all around there is a burgeoning of deliciously edible vegetation, honeybees and sweet-scented breezes which refresh and sustain your soul and your spirit, your mind and your body, with a delightful quickening energy which transforms all fatigue, restlessness and sorrow into a hallowed peace and a blessed wellbeing.

You hear the divine notes of mystical piping, and see the God and Goddess conjoined in their mystical dance between the trees beyond the Lake. In wonder you watch, and then you see the form of Krishna, beautiful beyond imagining, advancing towards you from the farther shores.

As he comes, the trees make an avenue for him by bending down their fruitful branches towards his feet. A ring of cuckoos take flight around his crown, and a higher one of doves encircle him from above.

The stags and roes and fauns of the deer folk rush up to meet him with devoted affection, and the honey bees make patterns in the air about him which match those of the mandala you saw reflected in the depths of the lake. Peacocks dance before him, and the songbirds warble and trill and dive in ecstasy through and through his aura.

Krishna comes to the very edge of the water and plays his pipe so that your heart is pierced by the loveliness of his essence. You notice a little boat below you, pulled up onto the white sands of the lake's margin.

You rise to your feet, entranced, and walk upon the magical shores of the Lake of Peace. In obedience to the silent command of Krishna, you climb into the boat.

As if charmed, it gently launches itself into the water, and you sail out into the midst of the lake, absorbing its perfect stillness and gentle serenity. Spend some moments gazing out across the calm, hushed waters.

You observe Krishna walking into the waters. He disappears beneath them, but you can still hear the sweet notes of his piping.

He rises in magnificence beside your boat, manifesting now as Vishnu, the Preserver, the protector of righteousness and the guardian of humanity.

Vishnu has taken the form of a fish or a merman, Matsya, and holds up his hands to bless you and to bring you peace.

'Come into the healing waters, my child,' he says to you, and in your body of light you leave the boat and find that you are bathing in the water, supported as if by unseen arms. It washes over you in a baptism of peace, and you see that your shining self is making the water sparkle with a streaming galaxy of perfect six-pointed stars which connect you to the holy life-force issuing from Matsya.

You notice that the water does not prevent you from breathing even when it closes momentarily over your head, but rather enhances it and frees your breath.

'Behold your boat,' says Matsya, and you turn your gaze upon it to find that sometimes it seems to hover above the surface of the water as if it were made of starlight with billowing silver sails; and sometimes it is the simple and humble boat you found upon the shore, except that strangely it seems made of flesh and sinks deeper into the water until half-submerged.

'When you are in your earthly boat,' Matsya says to you, 'and waves of turbulence come to you — waves of emotion, waves of distress, waves of anger and turmoil, waves of intolerance, waves of pain or fear, waves of cynicism and disgust with life and the swamping wave of non-endurance which follows all these — think of your shining self who is connected to Me at its heart and say these words or give out these thoughts:

'Peace, peace, peace to the violent waves which threaten to overwhelm me.

'Peace to the troubled brow, peace to the agitated breast, peace to the tormented solar plexus and to the fires below.

'Heart-peace, soul-peace, star-peace, tarashanti, be with me now in the name of the Great Spirit.

'Heart-peace, soul-peace, star-peace, tarashanti, encompass the world and bless the heart of every member of humanity.

'I dwell in silence and stillness within the gentle waters of the Lake of Peace where not a murmur, not a breath, disturbs the great heart of peace where the Spirit dwells.'

Matsya smiles upon you and pronounces his blessing over you:

'Perfect peace, profound peace, the still deeps of peace be forever your dwelling-place as you move through the illusions of chaos which try to shatter the earthly life of the soul. None shall assail you.

'Peace, peace, peace to you, dear one. Peace of the child within its Mother's arms, peace of the child within its Father's protection. Peace everlasting, peace ever-flowing, peace divine.'

The lake in the forest, its wonder, its secrets, its enchanted people and the presence of the Great Spirit, begins to recede within you, enfolded into the radiant jewel which is your heart. Come back gently, touch down in the mundane world, and carry these treasures within you.

Seal your centres with the bright silver cross in a ring of light.

Protecting Loved Ones

One of the most beautiful aspects of communing with our guardian angel is that we have been given the power to direct its protective presence to those in need. If we know of loved ones (or anyone in an emergency who may need help) we can speed our angel on wings of light to rescue and safeguard them. We can send love, protection, healing and comfort via our guardian angel. We need only to speak their name and ask our angel to go to their aid for it to be done instantly.

But what of their own guardian angel? The answer to this question seems to be that the guardian angels work together to create a field of protection for the human soul (or souls) in an emergency, calling in other angels as their aid is needed. It is particularly helpful to do this where the one in need has no conscious link with their own guardian angel, because in this case the necessary link to facilitate angelic guardianship is provided by you (see Chapter One).

If you send your guardian angel to help another, are you yourself left unprotected whilst the angel fulfils your request? Not at all! Angels are not restricted to the narrow dimensions of time, space and matter which imprison us, and they are still there at our side even whilst they travel through the ether at immeasurable speed to bring help to the person (or people) you have named.

There are three simple ways to begin to establish direct communion with your guardian angel. These will soon be overidden by
methods of your own once you are well on your way to a rich and
frequent inner dialogue, but they will be found helpful until this is
achieved.

1 Find a tree which is in harmony with your soul (pines are
   particularly blessed with light-consciousness). Place your
   hands upon its trunk and ask it to help you and your
   guardian angel to connect in full awareness. Go to the
   heart-centre and send a bright star of love and light to all
   humanity, to Mother Earth, her animals, and her world
   of nature, inviting your angel and the tree-spirit to help
   you in your work. Give your guardian angel time to align
   with you. Soon you will begin to feel its presence,
   normally behind you, enfolding you in its wings.

2 Spend five minutes each day listening and attuning to
   your angels. First, send your consciousness up your
   heavenly stairway to the Great Spirit, the Divine Source.
   Breathe in its blessing and begin to listen inwardly to the
   voice of your angel. Write down what it has to say.

3 Use the beautiful guardian angel prayers and invocations
   given in Chapter Three, which are from the Western Isles
   of Scotland (I have adapted them very slightly so that
   they are in tune with the concept of God as Father-
   Mother, Goddess-God). As you settle down to sleep,
   consciously prepare yourself by an act of prayer and
   aspiration to be released into the spiritual worlds in
   company with your guardian angel, who waits with
   patience, hope and loving kindness to receive you and
   unite with you on the other side of sleep.

It is worth remembering that we actually plan the forthcoming day
with our guardian angel in our sleep state. Each coming day is pro-
grammed for us – set with the jewels of aspiration, inspiration, and
spiritual and practical goals, by our angel, in counsel with our soul,

before it is entrusted to our care and it begins to unfold. Sadly, most people immediately overthrow their angel's blueprint on waking, subconsciously rebelling against the beautiful drafts and designs that would lead them to spread the wings of the soul and to mount to the high places within themselves. The whole point of our life on earth is to learn to overcome and transform this ruffian and vandal that destroys our link with the spiritual worlds.

To reconnect with your angel's scheme for the day, it is only necessary to perform a task, however simple, with heart-centredness. Give your full focus and concentration to the work in hand, and cultivate a sense of rest, ease and peace within – within the mind, within the emotions, within the nervous system – and then deeper, to your innermost heart.

When we do this, we can create sanctuaries within our day where our angel can rest in our thoughts, and so renew its link with us. It is a matter of gently insisting that your heart, your emotions, your spirits, rise into the temple of your being like incense, rather than allowing the heart, the mood, the mind, to sink into gloom, lethargy, discontent and distaste for life. When we lovingly insist that our being rises to its temple (and we are invested with that power to gently insist), our thoughts naturally create such angel sanctuaries, and the strategies of blessing, vision, and soul-architecture that our angel has created to facilitate the process of our gradual ascent into freedom are not frustrated.

—◌ A N G E L I C   S E E D · T H O U G H T S   ◌—

For He hath given his angels charge over thee,
to keep thee in all thy ways.

Psalm 90, The Book of Psalms

And these are the names of the holy angels who
   watch.

URIEL, one of the holy angels who is over the world
   and over Tartarus.

RAPHAEL, one of the holy angels who is over the
   spirits of men.

RAGUEL, one of the holy angels who takes
   vengeance on the world of the luminaries.

MICHAEL, one of the holy angels, to wit, he that is
   set over the best part of humankind and over
   chaos.

SARAQUEL, one of the holy angels who is set over
   the spirits who sin in spirit.

GABRIEL, one of the holy angels who is over
   Paradise and the serpents and the Cherubim.

REMIEL, one of the holy angels, whom God sets over
   those who rise.

Apocrypha — Dead Sea Scroll

CHAPTER SIX

BECOMING A VIRGIN

One of the most beautiful aspects of attuning to the great spirit of Mary Magdalene whilst Margaret Bailey and I were 'bringing through' her teachings was receiving the grace of her revelations regarding the chakras. The guardian angel is so intimately linked with the gentle unfoldment of our chakras, which, in turn, links us to our soul, that I would like to offer Mary's teaching* here, with special regard to the role of our guardian angel in helping us to ascend the 'seven steps' to our soul-temple. These 'seven steps' are the chakras themselves, magical and starlit and guarded by angels when we evoke their energies in the light of spiritual understanding.

Our guardian angel's great role is to assist us in opening the flowers of our chakras in safety and completion, so that each one is given a burgeoning life which expresses itself in distinctive colour, sound, fragrance and motion. When this takes place, we enter our own individual 'Garden of Eden', in which our tender spiritual core is shielded from the invasion of darkness – the shadow of the adversarial forces. Once we are released from the burden of this darkness, we become 'fully human' (a phrase coined in the extant part of Mary's gospel). The grand task of the guardian angel, then, is to give us the gift of our perfected humanity – the ultimate awakening.

The second part of this great work that our angel seeks to accomplish in its care of us is to link our consciousness to the stars so that we may master 'the final frontier' and conjoin heaven and earth within ourselves. The first simple steps along the path of this majestic plan are provided in the next chapter.

Our angelic guardian longs to dispel the sleep and the lethargy (sometimes referred to as 'the weight of Saturn') that oppress us and

*The information on the chakras, slightly different in emphasis and form, is also given in our book *The Secret Teachings of Mary Magdalene*, by Claire Nahmad and Margaret Bailey.

prevent us from experiencing the springing of the fountain of spiritual life deep within us, whose living waters are connected to the essence of the stars. Our angel does this by lighting our chakra system, as if with a sacred taper, from the supernal flame secreted at our heart-centre. Ultimately, the heart-flame, aided by the balancing and monitoring of our guardian angel, will ignite the sleeping serpent of light coiled, or imprisoned, in our base chakra, at the bottom of the spine.

As well as the heart-flame, this is the divine light with which every human being is entrusted as he or she comes into incarnation. It is the light which penetrates the deepest fastnesses of earth, of the material realm, but which must be connected again to the stars, from whence it came, taking with it, as it were, our whole consciousness, our entire being. The celestial light of the stars has a spiritual counterpart, which we call God. Once we thus unite heaven and earth within ourselves, we become 'fully human'. Therefore, the task of enlightening the chakras of its individual charge, which is vouchsafed to each guardian angel, is its most holy and glorious mission. Our angel is ever watchful, seeking and waiting on every opportunity to invest us with the mystical raiment which is our sublime birthright – the raiment of the soul; and the raiment of the soul is bestowed by cleansing, enlightening and awakening our chakras from the sacred point of the heart, via our own spiritual effort and the ministering offices of our guardian angel.

Before beginning this study, it is a good idea to learn how to protect yourself and your chakras. We do this by 'unfurling our wings'.

Unfurling Our Wings

Our wings run from the base of the brain to the base of the spine, but when opened (unfurled) they enclose all the body from the soul-star chakra to the earth-star chakra (from above our head to below our feet). Follow these instructions to unfurl them, and thereby enclose yourself in protection.

Ground yourself.

Connect the heart, throat and head chakras with a spiritual inflow of light. Just see the white or golden spiritual light flowing into your heart, rising to the throat-centre (in the hollow of the throat), then to the brow-centre (just above and between the eyes), and from there to the crown-centre (located in the middle of the brain at the top of the head).

Here, the flow of spiritual light will separate into two separate streams. The first will flow to the second part of the crown-centre, which is situated at the top of the forehead, in the middle; the second will flow into the chakra at the base of the brain. The whole effect is like a springing fountain. Practise this procedure a few times, and soon you will be able to set the fountain springing with a single thought-command, as if you snapped your fingers to conjure it into being, rather than laboriously going through the entire process each time you wish or need to unfurl your wings.

Breathe rhythmically and easily.

Sense your spine, with its spinning chakras radiant like flowers of light, like a ramrod or a sword of light, fixing you securely into the good earth. See your chakras and your spine all aglow with an influx of divine light.

All the way down your spine, little golden seed pods of light are bursting into wing-fibres.

Let them extend to each side, growing vertically.

Now they grow both vertically and horizontally into huge, full-length wings.

Waft them to and fro.

Wrap them right round yourself so that you are in a tower of light.

Seal all your chakras, from crown to base, with a bright silver cross in a ring of white or golden light. (Eventually, this can be done with a single thought-command.)

See yourself in your tower of light, and know that positive emanations only will be permitted to pass in and out of its enclosure. Anything injurious or negative will glance off it as if off a shield, and fall harmlessly away.

The feminine symbol of the tower is deeply associated with the chakras. When the energies within these centres are awakened and purified, the beautiful play of light and heightened consciousness that they evoke forms a tower around our being. The tower spins – because the chakras spin – and becomes a tower of clear, pure light. This is the essence of the soul, the beautiful crystalline body that, through its perfect translucence, like crystal, like water, like a mirror, reflects the supernal light of the spirit into the entity that is our individual being.

This is the true meaning of 'virgin'. It depicts a state whereby a person has, via the striving of their own higher will, purified the energies of the chakras through the experience of countless lives on earth, and has thereby become so attuned to the guidance of the spirit and the prompting of the soul that their enlightenment has become their nature, their natural response to all life's challenges. That tower of spinning crystalline light has become their 'habit', their raiment. Thus do we become 'virgin' – locked so securely into our tower of light that we are impregnable as far as the forces of darkness are concerned. Of course, the tower is not a prison, but rather a perfectly protected entry into boundless worlds of light.

Therefore, the tower itself *is* the 'virgin' – the emblem of unassailable spiritual strength, inviolable because it cannot be penetrated by the dark adversarial forces. It is the symbol and the actuality of the soul resplendent, glorious – victorious over the claims of the lower self. The symbols of ancient myth become easier to understand in this context, particularly in relation to Arianrhod, the spinning goddess whose ancient seat was the revolving crystal castle of Celtic and other legends.

We tend to think of the spinning goddesses (Arianrhod, Arachne, Ariadne and Isis, to name but a few) in relation to spinning and weaving flax or thread, which is an important factor in their mystical significance, for they are the goddesses of destiny in their role as queen and mistress of the soul, producing the magical thread or clew (clue) out of their own essence that leads each human soul through the labyrinth and pitfalls of earthly life to the sunlit summits of spiritual freedom. Just as significant, however, is the concept of spinning as the rotation of the planets and the stars; all creation spins; and it is these revolutions which carry us through space and time until our dance leads us past the threshold of the heavenly worlds and into the divine motion of the realm of 'the imperishable stars'.

It is for this greater destiny that our guardian angel has been appointed to us, to guide us and keep us on our own individual path towards that measurelessly precious birthright which has been granted to every human soul. Although the guardian angel will attend with scrupulous care to the smallest detail of our everyday lives, it is well to keep in mind its grand mission and vision for us, so that we do not minimize or undermine the beauty and the mystery of our guardian angel's relationship with us, or become so mired in the pettiness of the 'bestial floor' (our earthly life in an animal body) that we mistakenly come to think of our guardian angel as a personal servant, rather than a server of Love and its ineffable plan. Through our chakras does our angel speak with and enlighten us; and so it is with the chakras that we can work to facilitate and evoke blessings upon that relationship.

It is also good to begin your work on your chakras (which will be dynamic and transformative) with a prayer to the great Angel of Wisdom, Sophia. Sophia is deeply linked to both Brigid and Mary Magdalene, and these three Sisters of Light form the triple goddess, the loving face of Divine Mother. You may like to use the following prayer.

ANGEL PRAYER

Great Angel of Wisdom, Sophia,

I request your presence today,

To bless me and to empower that within me

Which is Divine.

Strengthen my sacred link

With the Great Mother of All;

Strengthen my links of light

With my angel guardian;

And let me rise to meet my true destiny

As a woman,*

An expression of the Spirit of Wisdom.

Now I see you before me,

Emitting a great light,

So still, so beautiful,

In your crimson cloak

And your robes of gentle blue,

Shining with stars.

I am enfolded

In your bright white and golden light.

I am deeply blessed and protected,

Guided and enlightened.

I am ushered into the Heart

Of Divine Mother

As the dewdrop slips into the ocean.

I thank you, dear Sophia,

And ask you to always be with me.

May Brigid, Sophia and Mary Magdalene,

Sisters three to all humanity

Be my guiding light!

Amen!

The Mystery of the Vivaxis

In considering our chakras, we need to take into account the pioneering work of Frances Nixon, who discovered the phenomenon of the Vivaxis, described as our 'energy point of origin'. (See *The Vivaxis Connection* by Judy Jacka.) By careful and meticulous research, she proved that we are connected throughout life by lines of energy to our Vivaxis sphere. Frances Nixon gave it this name from an amalgamation of the Latin words *viva* (life) and *axis* (which is a central line around which a rotating body moves) because her observations revealed that the life force of each individual rotated about this central point that is the Vivaxis.

The Vivaxis is a little sphere, the size of a foetus, which is usually formed in the last few weeks of a pregnancy, when the incoming soul has finally 'touched base' and has arrived securely in the body of the unborn baby (although it actually takes 21 years to thoroughly 'ground' the soul in the physical body, which is the inner reason why we associate our 21st birthday with 'coming of age'). At this point, the little Vivaxis sphere is released into the earth and fixes there, generally at some spot where the mother lived or spent time in the final few weeks of gestation. There it faithfully remains, however far its owner travels from the site of its location.

Frances Nixon explains that the atomic particles inside the Vivaxis energy sphere align themselves with, and become magnetized to, the geophysical field in which the Vivaxis 'earths' itself.

*Alternatively: 'the Sacred Feminine Principle within me'

This magnetizing of the energies causes a wave link to establish itself between the Vivaxis sphere and its owner which remains constant regardless of distance.

There is a bilateral flow of energy between ourselves and our Vivaxis. The energy flow coming to us from the Vivaxis travels vertically until it reaches our current altitude, then horizontally until it reaches our left foot, switching to a vertical flow once again as it moves up our left leg to our left hand. The flow of energy returns to the Vivaxis sphere via a vertical direction through our right foot up to our right hand, wherefrom it flows in an outgoing horizontal direction from our right hand.

It is well worth studying the mysteries of the Vivaxis and applying them to our lives. The discovery of the Vivaxis is indeed remarkable, and I believe it has a direct connection to our chakra system.

Although it seems likely that there are twelve major chakras, most people currently work only with seven. These correspond to the seven astrological spheres, which are expressions of the seven rays of creation. Esotericists believe that creation itself *is* music – the mystery of the Word issuing forth from the divine source. If so (and there exists all kinds of evidence, from many varying disciplines, to support this concept), we can see that the seven astrological 'planets', the seven main chakras and the seven steps up the pyramid of our inner being to our soul-temple at the pinnacle, equate to the seven tones of music which together form an octave – a 'plane' or a 'level' of creation.

However, the seven tones alone do not create the octave. This comes into being when the first tone of one harmonic (seven notes) is in harmony with the first tone of the next harmonic. In fact, these two notes are the same, only the higher obviously vibrates at a faster rate than the lower. And so we see that the seven tones, or the seven rays, permeate every level and every facet of creation, and that the scale is ever ascending in higher and yet higher octaves, each more heavenly than that preceding it. The octave upon which we exist seems to be the lowest and the slowest, the furthest removed from the divine source.

As we can see, the seven and the one work in harmony to create each sphere or level, which gives a highly significant distinction to the number eight. Many traditions attribute deep holiness and mystery to the number eight. Its serpentine form is considered to represent infinity. It seems that a method of understanding this mystery is to see ourselves as individual souls, and the planet earth, as the 'eighth' note of the sphere of creation we inhabit. She is therefore the outward expression of the level or the plane we inhabit – the planetary sphere itself, and its ever-unfolding dimensions. We are the one and the seven, the eighth, the octave, a unit of harmony in the symphony of creation. It was revealed to Margaret Bailey and me that Mary Magdalene herself embodied the mystery of eight.

It is very interesting, in this context, to consider what the 'eighth' main chakra might be. Now that the Vivaxis has been discovered, it seems that we may have the answer.

The chakras that Mary is guiding us to develop are those in the hands and the feet. From one perspective, these would seem to be four chakras (four, or the cube, is the sacred sigil for the earth). Yet, perhaps, all these four are actually only *one* chakra – the earth chakra. This idea becomes more exciting when we consider that we can actually see the colour of this eighth ray for ourselves.

We know that the seven rays are demonstrated to us in the reflective beauty of the rainbow; yet the rainbow is only half a circle. The resonant sphere of creation that is the octave is permeated throughout its structure by the seven rays or tones, but it needs the 'eighth' ray or tone to complete it (the eighth ray being, in reality, the first ray or tone of the next, higher octave, but yet possessing its own mysterious identity and characteristics, which unite in the great theme of *connection*; and here we have the clue as to why eight represents eternity: it *connects* all the spheres of creation, and is in itself, therefore, the principle of eternity). If you take a CD and examine its surface, you will see the seven rays of the rainbow faithfully reflected therein; but you will also catch sight of the eighth ray, because the CD is a perfect circle, and not an incomplete rendition of it, as is the rainbow.

This ray is *magenta* in colour (we like the apparently random association with 'Magdalene'!), and it is the eighth ray; the earth ray.

If the Earth is in herself the expression of the octave created by the 'eighth' ray, we would expect the earth ray to express the red colour of the first tone or ray of the first octave, and the lighter (faster in vibration) red colour of the first tone or ray of the higher octave, which completes the first octave. And, indeed, this is so; we have in magenta the blending of the deep red of the first tone, and the lighter red of the higher tone. The harmonizing of these two colours gives us a rich pink hue.

But magenta is more than a rich, rosy pink; it has a touch of violet in it. And, according to the theory under examination, this makes perfect sense, because of course the last ray of the seven is the colour violet; and although the eighth ray begins the next octave over again on a higher harmonic, and so consistently is a form of the red ray, the octave as a complete sphere in itself consists of the harmonized perfection of the seven rays, which begin with red and end with violet. Therefore, we would expect that the earth ray, the eighth ray, would be a harmonized blending of red, lighter red, and violet – forming magenta.

This special eighth ray, then, denotes the first and the last, the alpha and the omega. It is connected to the red base chakra – the first ray – and yet it transcends even the crown-centre, the violet ray (although, as we shall see, the chakras do not conform rigidly to the seven colours of the rainbow, even if there is an undoubted correspondence). It is the ray of connection and harmony. And these are precisely the qualities that we intuited were associated with the chakra (because I believe it really is one chakra, complete in itself) that is active in our hands and feet.

We can help to activate and to purify this eighth chakra of the hands and the feet by consciously connecting with our Vivaxis. Just think of the little sphere of your Vivaxis, the same size as you were when in your foetal stage, so precious because it declares beyond contradiction that you contain the earth within yourself, that you *are* the octave which is the vibration of the earth sphere; and, therefore, you hold the destiny and the future of the earth in your hands.

The eighth chakra of the hands and the feet needs further investigation; but for now, we can begin to develop it simply and harmlessly with the help of our Vivaxis.

Finding Our Vivaxis

Take two pendulums, or objects on a chain. Hold one chain in each hand.

Stand erect, with feet apart, your heels touching, (so that a V shape is created between your feet).

Gently turn clockwise, a few degrees at a time.

Note the motion of the chains in your hand. When they swing back and forth in alternating movements, you are aligned with your Vivaxis. (If the chains swing in unison, you are standing at right angles to it.)

Once you have aligned your body with your Vivaxis, you can carry out the following exercise:

Stand quietly, without holding either pendulum, and begin to be aware that you are receiving a flow of energy from your Vivaxis. It is coming in beneath your left foot, travelling up your left leg, and entering your left hand. Just feel this for a moment or two.

Now sense the Vivaxis energy crossing the trunk of your body between the solar plexus and the sacral chakras. As it does so, the energy connects with your navel, and then carries on down the inside of your right leg until it enters your right foot. From there, it climbs the outside of your right leg until it enters your right hand. It is at this point that the energy flows back to your Vivaxis; so the outgoing energy becomes the returning flow as it enters the right foot and travels back up the right leg to the right hand, at which point it actually leaves the body.*

When you have a clear sense of the direction and the circulation of the Vivaxis energy, open your right hand, slightly cupping the palm, and call on your guardian angel. Ask it to oversee this exercise.

Using your breath, drawing it through your heart, and using the clear visualization of the star in the heart, send bright white starlight, of a beautiful, pristine, coruscating purity, out with the Vivaxis energy leaving your right hand. Say to your angel: 'Guardian angel (or its name), please bring all safely into balance and harmony; please circulate the white light seven times throughout me and my Vivaxis. Please bless, protect and stabilize my earth chakra.'

Visualize the beautiful white starlight coming back into your left foot with the Vivaxis energy; and then watch it flow in and out, to complete the circuit seven times.

Ask for the blessing of Mary, Sophia, Brigid, and Divine Mother and her angels, on your earth chakra.

Thank your guardian angel for its help.

Don't neglect the actual visualization of the light. Angels and humans work together, and it is not fair (or effective) to leave all the work to our guardian angel!

After performing these exercises, become aware, in your daily life, of your hands as agents of blessing. We do almost everything with our hands, and they can become powerful tools for transforming our lives, and even the world. The chakras in our palms can

---

*As I wrote this exercise, I received the strong impression that people who receive the stigmata (where the hands and feet mysteriously bleed) are actually expressing an earth-memory of the Crucifixion through their earth chakra. Margaret Bailey and I were told that this event was so traumatic for the earth spirit that it was locked into her soul-memory as a vivid impress of compassion and suffering. Those who, operating upon a certain frequency, open their hearts to suffering in attunement with the compassion of Christ, receive the outward expression of this earth-memory through their Vivaxis by bleeding from their hands and feet. This would explain why the bleeding is from the very centre of the soles and palms (scoffers are convinced that stigmata sufferers are merely hysterical, because the nails of the cross entered Christ's hands at the point of the wrist, not the palms, even though they evince no signs of nervous hysteria, and some of them are not even Christian!). It is at the very centre of the soles and the palms that the inflow and the outflow of our Vivaxis enters and leaves the body. If this is the explanation of the stigmata (and, considering the sacredness of the earth chakra and its electromagnetic manifestation – the Vivaxis – it seems that it must be), it is likely that stigmata sufferers would need to heal themselves via the means of the earth chakra and the Vivaxis.

bless, heal, caress, soothe, purify and create. Our feet, likewise, can walk gently on the earth – and they can dance! When we learn the rhythm of life, we will want to dance upon the earth much more than we do today. I believe that, as our earth chakra awakens and becomes active, we will all be dancing, young and old; not so much in night clubs and in dance halls, but unrestrained and free, out in the open air!

Investigations have only just begun regarding the earth chakra, so information regarding its fascinating dimensions are limited. However, Mary's teachings regarding the rest of the octave (the seven main chakras) and our guardian angel, can be given more comprehensively.

In preparation, you might like to try the following guided visualization concerning the Tree of Life, for that is what our chakras veritably are. Some traditions see them as the blooms upon a rose tree. Others associate them with the great World Ash, underlying the structure of every level of life. The Druids associated them with the oak. Whichever tree we prefer, it will always represent the spine, the sword of truth which connects us to the earth and the heavens, with the chakras flowering like roses or galaxies from its stem.

Meditation – The Tree of Life

Assume a relaxed meditative posture, making sure that you are comfortable and that your spine is erect and supported if necessary.

Connect with your heart-centre, begin to breathe gently 'through the heart' and feel your mind gradually becoming still and serene.

Begin to see a softly radiant angelic form take shape before you. It is a mighty angel, yet its presence is comforting and reassuring. It adapts its cosmic dimensions to the eyes of your soul, and you see that it is manifesting a female orientation.

Her robes are a cascade of white light over which the hues of the rainbow reflect and play in subtle shimmering

tones, ever-changing in myriad variants of the seven colour-
rays. Look into her eyes, serene as blue summer skies, and
let the realization wash through you that this is the Angel
of Peace.

She takes you by the hand so that you step forward out of
your limited everyday self and slip away with her through
the shining mists of dimension into the angelic worlds.

You have come to a celestial earth, free from the constrictions of space-matter-time that encircle the physical earth,
which has passed away from your awareness like a shadow
and a sigh and a fleeting dream. Now you behold the earth
of true reality.

It emanates such a flood of brilliant light that you can
hardly register what you see before you until the angel
begins to speak in a voice of calming quietude as soothing
as the hush of fairweather tides. She speaks directly to you,
and as her words form, the light becomes lucid, and clear
images begin to rise and fall softly on your spiritual sight.

'Come with me, Dweller in the Green World, down into the
deep secret places of the Earth, down deep into her Heart.
Here there is a great Light which glows like no outer sun,
but rather blazes with a spiritual light so pure and lovely
that mortal eyes may behold it only in dreams and visions
of the spirit. It is the brilliant effulgence of Love and Joy,
the supreme radiance of the Divine.

'Here in the Earth's Heart it is as if we stand in a paradise
garden; and in the Garden there grows a Tree. It is the Tree
of Life. We may go to it and stand at its great gnarled roots,
which wind away in all directions like petrified serpents.
How firmly anchored they are in the stuff of Mother Earth!

'Gaze up in wonder, Human Soul, into its fragrant boughs,
garlanded in leaves tenderly glowing with a soft, peaceful,
green hue, and hung with fruits of heavenly, scintillating
colours sparkling with the lustre of the stars. Rainbow-
coloured birds come and go among its branches, as do little
birds of gentle dun earth-shades, and strange mythic
animals whose fabulous colour and form you have never

seen or imagined before. Each one speaks to our heart and is our brother, our sister. In joyous communion we greet one another, and our voices rise in song, for it is the Morning of the New Day.

'Yes, the dawn is breaking and, as we look up, further and deeper into the Mysteries of the Tree, we see that there are many paths upwards into its boughs, as though it were all at once a Tree and a Mountain and our soul's deepest Dream.

'In delight our hearts take wing because we see that, at its very summit, the Light of the great Spirit streams forth and pours downward like a bright river of paradise deep into the Heart of the Earth where we stand, and into our own heart-vessels and into the world of sorrow below. Do you not see, Human Soul, that this great Tree of Life has roots not only at its base but also at its crown, and that these crown-roots are nourished by supernal worlds which may seem to you as if they vibrate at a measureless distance, but which I tell you do not lie far beyond but rather embrace the physical earth?

'Now in a vision within a vision, we see ourselves moving upwards upon two of the paths which lead from the roots, up to the heavens where the Shining Ones that you call angels choir in a wonder of bliss to help and inspire you on our upward way — yours to struggle in a tomb of flesh, ours to inhabit a radiant atmosphere pulsing with Creation's joy. There is a beautiful reason that this is so, and through it a triumph to be won which is beyond imagining.

'Do not wonder, Earth Child, on beholding that path parallel to your own. It is the path I tread, the beauty-path of the angels, for just as we descend from the heights so must we also ascend again. Angels too have a path of evolution blessed by the Tree. We are always with you and we can share worlds whenever you reach out to us and seek our presence.

'With the Staff of Life, the Pouch of Provisions and the

Undying Lantern we climb, and we are never alone. Around us, everyone upon their own elected path, we see the sons and daughters of Humanity and the sons and daughters of Faery ascending likewise; the path of Faery is a never-ending dance of the Earth's delight, for your feet also if you will tread it.

'Your paths cross and interweave. Fairy, angel and human beings are all linked in a Network of Light. And see how the birds of the Tree alight and dart and give forth music! They know no thresholds, but are dwellers in all three spheres.

'Now we are alone again, with the peaceful Tree stretching above us, waving its beautiful branches over our heads in benediction. Soothed, we dwell upon its shelter and protection, its kindly power and strength, the motherly perfume of its fruits and flowers, the lullabies in its rustling leaf-songs.

'Look carefully, Human Soul, for ten ineffable blossoms of the Mystical Rose are beginning to appear upon the Tree, and within each exquisite formation of fragrant petals is a winged figure. They are the Ten Divine Attributes of the perfected ManWoman, called Adam Kadmon.

'Ponder these things, for the secret of the winged figures at the heart of the blooms is one of liberation and peace for all creation.'

The Angel of Peace falls silent, and you see that she is becoming absorbed into the Tree. You understand that in a sense she is the Tree, its great supporting dynamic; and you realize that the essence of the Angel of Peace is Balance. She balances all the Ten Divine Attributes upon the Tree, and that is why she is truly the Angel of Peace.

In deep quietude, she gives you her blessing.

Refreshment of soul and gladness of heart steal over you. You stroke the bark of the Tree and feel its goodness, its wholeness. Rest contemplatively beneath its spreading green boughs for a while and consider the teaching that the great Angel of Peace has offered to you as her gift.

Balance in all things is the secret of peaceful living, for all suffering is a deprivation of balance. You realize that the Tree, with its great temple-like pillars, balances all creation and that every soul is given the opportunity to express the sacred principle of that Golden Mean of perfect balance, if it so wishes.

You look again upon the Tree of Life, and see the Angel of Peace as a quiet pulse emitting her essence from its heart. The revelation comes to you that the Tree of Life is also the Tree of Peace.

Comforted, healed and ready for renewed service, you seek once more the mundane earth of physicality below, taking with you the vivifying Light of the New Day.

Feel the solid ground beneath your feet, slowly refocus upon the things that surround you, and seal your centres.

Affirm:

'All the help I need to balance my inner and outer life is available to me. I only have to ask to receive it.

'The Angel of Peace is in my heart and builds her temple over me.

'The roots of the Tree of Life are ever at my feet and at my crown to give me strength and peace whenever I need to draw on them.'

The Tree of Life meditation dwells on the Ten Divine Attributes, which are the focus of the mystical Judaic Kabbala system. I suspect that, as in the case of the 'Ten' Commandments, there are actually twelve Divine Attributes, and that these are a part of the ever-unfolding mystery of the chakras.

The Base Chakra

The base of the pyramid that is the mystical structure of our greater being, and which we need to ascend to reach and to fully inhabit our soul-temple, equates to the world of matter into which we descend at birth. This four-square base represents our first main chakra, located at the base of the spine. It is symbolic of the physical life and the four elements which compose it.

The base chakra is linked with the planet Saturn, the constrainer and lawgiver. The mystery of the base chakra is contained in the stars of the constellation Capricorn and reflected in Aquarius. Its colour is fiery, volcano-red. It is connected with the sense of smell, its element is earth, it is associated with Merlin and the Crone (the wise old man and the wise old woman), and its challenges are Fear and Darkness. Saturn locks the Divine Light into this base chakra, holding it securely for us until the soul is ready, from the 'nous' or the point of light in our heart, to summon it up the spine and through the heart. From here it rises on three levels with the grace and beauty of a fountain, springing from the throat, the brow and the crown chakras. As it rises, it awakens and vivifies the chakras in turn until each one becomes a brilliant gyroscope of light, colour and sound, permeated by the exquisite energies of the spiritual worlds.

When we have learned the lessons of the base chakra, we find ourselves on the first step of the seven leading up to the summit of the pyramid. We have overcome the dark sleep of unawareness and our journey has begun. Nevertheless, we are still at the level of the base chakra; it is just that now we are aware of it! The fire of consciousness has opened an eye, and we ascend from the sleep of the elements (the physical body only aware of its animal nature) to the first step of the awareness of our spiritual nature. Again, we must overcome darkness and fear, but this time at a more subtle level.

The strength, wisdom, endurance and longevity of the elephant is associated with the base chakra, and with the lessons we must learn upon this first level. The idea that the elephant 'never forgets' is an essential principle of the school of the base chakra. We must never allow ourselves to fall back into the sleep of unawareness which is induced by the lull of the earth plane, or we will find ourselves faced with the repetition of all its rigorous lessons. Its ultimate lesson is that of service, teaching us to override the basic earthly and animalistic instinct to look after 'number one' and pursue self-serving aims, and, with the help of the soul, to transmute survival into the ideal of service. This choice, then, to replace purely self-serving aims with service to what is Higher – in ourselves and in all beings – is fundamental to the spiritual path. Without this first step, no others can be taken. It is the very doorway to the Divine.

To assist us in learning the lessons of the base chakra, to help us to manifest its perfected qualities and to overcome its great obstacles of darkness and fear, our guardian angel will link us to angels of courage and perseverance, of truth and enlightenment, of service and synthesis, to the angels of wisdom and to the mighty Angel of Achievement. It will always do this via your heart chakra, even though you are working with your first chakra, because the essential point of balance lies in the heart. (We must ensure that we always work from our heart when unfolding our chakras, for our own safety and wellbeing.) We need to make time to sit with our guardian angel and to ask for this work to be done on our behalf. We must never forget to ask, because without this invitation, and without consciously opening up to our guardian angel, its ability to help us is severely restricted.

When you are troubled by feelings of fear and darkness (the latter manifests as confusion, depression, constant weariness, feelings of inner sightlessness – all that bears a heavy, dark aspect and oppresses the soul), use the symbol of the Rose, lit at its core by the jewel of the spirit, to ease your anxieties and to dispel your darkness (also, if you wish, The Spirit of the Rose meditation given in Chapter Two). Concentrate particularly on the sweet, cleansing, healing perfume of the Rose. When you use the Rose as a meditative symbol specifically to help you to overcome the fear and darkness of the base chakra, call in your guardian angel on the task. Let it be there in your meditation; it will carry the receptacle of your thoughts, your prayers and your aspirations upwards to catch the light of heaven, and will bless, quicken and purify the indwelling light within your base chakra. It will help you to feel the wonderful reassurance and protection of Divine Mother, and the sweet, scintillating touch of the angels of joy.

Our guardian angel's message to us in helping us to overcome the challenges of the base chakra might be given as: 'Take heart, stay focused, and keep on looking up.'

The Sacral Chakra

The second step of the pyramid is the sacral chakra, a little below the navel. This chakra is associated with the planet Jupiter. Its mystery is contained in the stars of the constellation Pisces and is reflected in Sagittarius. Its colour is glorious orange shot through with crimson. It is connected with the sense of taste, its element is water, and it is associated with the gods and goddesses of humour, expansion, benevolence and exploration. The lesson of the second chakra is that of overcoming desire and addiction, those hooks of the lower self, and attaining the resultant gifts of peace and wisdom.

In Mary's gospel (the gnostic Gospel of Mary) it is explained that the force of desire uses the soul as a garment, making a body out of her so that it can express its own unappeasable nature. It harries, drives and exhausts the soul, never recognizing her presence but concerned exclusively with its own power to dominate this 'body' that it unconsciously assumes. When the soul will collude no more with this unconsciousness of herself, she arises and withdraws authority from the urgent claims of desire, asserting her own power of command. Desire is first outraged and unbelieving, then silenced into submission. Henceforth, the soul will summon, modify or dismiss desire as her wisdom, working through the law of love, deems appropriate.

This chakra is associated with the generative organs and with the expression of creative energy at the etheric level of life emanating from thought-power and imagination. All forms of procreative power must express the law of love, otherwise they become predatory and destructive.

An important centre connected with the sacral chakra is the spleen. The old saying 'sacrificing to spleen' (destroying something in a petulant rage that might be regretted later) is an apt verbal depiction of the overwhelming, inundating tendencies of the untransmuted energies of the sacral centre.

The animal of this chakra is the alligator, which can manifest as the powerful and dangerous predator of the waters, or as the sacred dragon (which the alligator or crocodile represents in some pantheons, especially that of ancient Egypt). And the dragon, of course, is symbolic of the Dragon Queen, rumoured of in myth as 'she who bore them all', who brings the great currents of life to humanity and the physical realm and who is merciful, wise and all-encompassing in her love.

When working with this chakra (from the point of the heart), ask your guardian angel to link you with the angels of renunciation and regeneration, the angels of patience and acceptance, and the great Angel of Peace. To allow the Angel of Peace to draw very close, practise a breathing meditation (see Chapter One) and, if you feel inclined, The Lake of Peace meditation (see Chapter Five). Invite your guardian angel to breathe with you, even though it breathes an air subtler than the physical. Through your cleansing, harmonizing breath, your guardian angel will enter you and bring blessing, healing and cleansing to the spiritual light in your sacral chakra.

Our guardian angel's message to us in helping us to overcome the challenges of the sacral chakra might be given as: 'Learn to laugh at yourself and your extremes; but always laugh kindly.'

The Solar Plexus Chakra

The third stair of the pyramid is mounted via the solar plexus chakra. This is linked with the planet Mars, the warrior and the achiever. Its mystery is contained in the stars of the constellation Aries, and is reflected in Scorpio. Its colour ranges from green to golden green to warm, rich gold. It is connected with the sense of sight, its element is air, and it is associated with gods and goddesses

of courage, victory and willpower, those divinities who bless the
questing soul and the pioneer. The great lesson of the third chakra
is love, in both its human and divine aspects. Its challenge is ignorance.

There is a strong link between the solar plexus chakra and the
sacral or second chakra. A large network of nerves connect the two
centres, and both are associated with the desire nature. The desire
nature of the Sacred Feminine is emphasized in the second chakra,
which is connected to the moon by its element: water; but it reflects
itself in fire – the reflected fire which is that of the lower nature.
The desire nature of the Sacred Masculine is emphasized in the solar
plexus centre, which is linked to the air element. In this instance,
the air of the solar plexus chakra, manifesting as Ignorance, can
tend to oxygenate the reflected fire of the desire nature emanating
from the sacral chakra. Thus the second and third chakras contain
the lunar and solar energies of the desire-body which, when
overcome (as Jesus says in Mary's gospel, 'All aspects have to be
overcome'), metamorphose into peace, wisdom and love. Joan
Hodgson, in her book, *The Stars and the Chakras*, confirms this when
she teaches that 'There is a close connection between the [fire-
feeding] solar plexus centre and the frontal mind, both being
associated with Mars.'

The animal traditionally belonging to the solar plexus chakra is
the ram, the beast of sacrifice, for the lower fires must be sacrificed
to the divine flame in the heart. The desire nature has to willingly
offer itself in sacrifice and shut down the misuse of the air element,
manifesting as the bellows of ignorance feeding the fires of wrath.
When this damper is applied to ignorance and the mystery of air is
used correctly, which is to connect us to the higher mind (the
'nous') that feeds the holy flame of the Spirit, then those dangerous
reflected or astral fires are transfigured into the blessing of the divine
light of the Godhead, and the ram, baptized in its radiance, attains
its golden fleece.

When working with this chakra, ask your guardian angel to link
you to the angels of victory and triumph, the angels of humility and
sacrifice, and the Angel of Illusion and Reality. You will also need to

work with the Angel of Peace, the Angel of Wisdom, and the Angel of Love.

Meditate on the star in the heart (see page 12), and perform a breathing meditation. If you wish, you can also use the Temple of the Sun meditation (see Chapter Four). Invite your guardian angel into your meditation, and it will blend with the light in your heart to attune, bless and irradiate the spiritual light in your solar plexus chakra.

Our guardian angel's message to us in helping us to overcome the challenges of the solar plexus chakra might be given as: 'Let the consciousness in your solar plexus say, "I bend my knee and serve the heart."'

The Heart Chakra

The fourth stair up the pyramid of our greater self is the heart chakra. It is, of course, the centre of our being, our sun-self around which our being revolves. This chakra is linked with the sun, the golden, perfected being, the Son-Daughter of Goddess-God, and its element is fire. The mystery of the heart chakra is contained in the stars of the constellation Leo and reflected in Cancer. Its colour is a calm, radiant clear gold merging into brilliant wine-red. It is connected with the sense of feeling and touch, its lesson is the ultimate expression of Love – universal brotherhood – and its challenge, according to Mary's gospel, is Lethal Jealousy or Fear of Death.

It is in the heart that the point of balance between darkness and light is found – the 'nous' which connects the soul and the spirit and which lies between the two. It is the solvent of conflict. There is a rainbow bridge which connects the heart and the head centres and which extends beyond the crown chakra, a bridge which leads from earth to heaven and from heaven to earth. At both ends of the rainbow (the earth end being our human heart and the heaven end being our connection to the Divine) there lies buried a cup, the Rainbow Chalice. One of the cups (the heart) receives and the other (our divine self) gives forth. When we pass through the 'nous', the chalice that we bear in our heart becomes magically endowed and gives forth as well as receiving. The rainbow bridge is the 'nous', and it is there that the chalice or the Holy Grail dwells. 'Where the nous is, there lies the treasure.' (The Gospel of Mary – a gnostic text).

The guardians of the temple of the heart are Venus, Mercury and Saturn. Saturn is the Alpha of the spine, Mercury is the Omega. At its midpoint, reflecting the heart-sun, is Venus, planet of love and harmony. Saturn, the lawgiver, ensures that the heart obeys the Law of Love. Mercury, at the top of the spine, is linked with Archangel Raphael (Merlin or Saturn in another guise). Mercury is also Robin Hood, not lawless but an outlaw (outside the law), the golden con-sciousness that has transcended the constricting chains of Saturn because his lessons have been learnt and the law is within his heart. It can no longer imprison him. Venus is the point of balance between the two, the ascended soul who remains alive in a physical body on earth. This is the ultimate goal of the heart – to spiritualize the earth itself, and exalt brotherhood to the point of celestial harmony.

When the heart is unaware of its royal lineage (the connection it has to the Godhead) the vision of the soul fails, and it believes that the life beating in its heart is purely physical and will pass away. The soul clings to the fear of death and cannot find its unity, its at-one-ment with others. It equates ego with life and needs to feel that others are less than itself. This creates lethal jealousy, the antithesis of brotherhood. The heart that bears true knowledge of the 'nous' will never make this fatal mistake.

Now we can see why the animal associated with the heart is the sphinx. This creature represents supreme consciousness rising from an animal body set four-square on the earth, as is the base of the mystical pyramid whose qualities, through the chakras, we are exploring; and in its most mystical aspect it signifies the fused being of the Spirit and the Bride (represented on earth by Jesus and Mary Magdalene) – the heart-centre itself.

Meditate with your guardian angel on the Chalice, or the Holy Grail. (You may also like to use the meditation on the Sacred and Eternal Flame given in Chapter Two), and your angel will gently assist you to open your heart-centre. Ask your angel to link you to the angels of unconditional love and freedom, and the Angel of

Abundance. Your angel will also link you with Archangel Michael and his consort (an angelic reflection of the Bride).

Our guardian angel's message to us in helping us to rise to the challenges of the heart chakra might be given as: 'Never let your heart chakra close off and hide its light; and remember that when your consciousness radiates from this centre, you are the divine "I Am".'

The Throat Chakra

The fifth stair upon the pyramid represents the throat chakra. This centre is linked with the planet Venus, the planet of love, harmony and beautiful creation. Its mystery is contained in the stars of the constellation Taurus and is reflected in Libra. Its colour is fiery gold transforming into vivid lilac or ultraviolet. It is connected with the sense of hearing and listening, its element is the white ether from which all form is brought into being and is also the space in which it is contained, and it is associated with Brigid or Bride (the Daughter) and Divine Mother, the Great Goddess herself. Its lesson is that of harmonious union, and its challenge is the power of the flesh, or enslavement to the body.

Venus and Mercury work together to vivify the higher centres (the heart, the throat, the brow and crown chakras) and Mercury's influence is certainly strong in the fifth centre. But we may think of Venus as bringing us the Silence, that sphere of clarifying peace which actually opens our ears that we might hear. ('Those who have ears, let them hear' is used as a refrain by Jesus many times throughout Mary's gospel.) Until we enter the Silence, we cannot really hear or listen.

On entering the Silence to commune with Mary, Margaret Bailey was initially given a stalk of wheat from the hands of this exalted and loving presence. On contemplating this, we thought that the wheat was a sign of Mary Magdalene as the Bread of Life, and that it linked her with the star sign of the Virgin, meaning that the greater soul of Mary Magdalene who is the Dragon Queen actually holds dominion over virgin matter, the white ether which is the Thread of Life and from which all material form is spun and woven.

Upon the stalk of wheat which the Virgin holds, and upon that given to Margaret, are clustered five ears. These five ears of wheat also link Virgo with the five-pointed star of Venus or the penta-gram, associated with the secret elixir or Quintessence of the alchemists. Whereas the ancient Greeks declared that there were four elements in which matter could exist, the Pythagoreans added a fifth: the element of ether, purer and more subtle than fire and endowed with an orbicular motion. Ether was said to have flown upwards at creation and to have formed the stars as the fifth essence (the quintessence), the most subtle and refined extract of a body that can be procured.

Such a magical notion inspired the alchemists whose task it was to discover the spirituality in nature and matter; so they created essences 'five times distilled' as an esoteric principle. The ancient Roman author Horace links Venus with the Earth Goddess, Divine Mother and the Virgin (in Virgo) when he speaks of 'kisses which Venus has imbued with the quintessence of her own nectar'.

The genesis of Virgo, the stellar goddess studded with stars, is found in ancient Egypt where the Corn Maiden (Virgo) is none other than Isis herself, her dress flowing with stars, holding either a wand of office (interchangeable with the distaff, symbol of the Spinning Woman, as her office is to weave creation) or her child, Horus, who represents the Eye of God. This eye is always portrayed singly and is a symbol of the Third Eye, that centre of consciousness which is said to lead from earthly understanding to divine apper-ception of the cosmos. (It is worth noting that when Margaret is led into the sphere of Silence, her outlook is always that of the starry heavens.) So Venus, Isis and the Corn Maiden of Virgo are one; they are all associated with spinning and weaving, they are all asso-ciated with the fifth element of ether and the stars, and they are all associated with Mary Magdalene.

The throat chakra is linked with the element ether and with formulating the Word that began all creation ('In the beginning was the Word', John's gospel tells us – John, who was the actual and mystical brother of Mary). It is connected with the achievement of harmonious union, a union that cannot come about until our ability to communicate with one another is harmonized in the heart. This idea of harmonious communication is symbolized by the spider's web, a network of 'etheric lines of communication' often created in an octagonal shape, at the heart of which sits the eight-rayed being, the Spinner and Weaver. The idea of harmony is contained in the number eight, which represents the octave.

Could it be that enslavement to the flesh, meaning the inability to free our consciousness from the mundane plane and its limited conceptions and so realize the wonder of our origins and the glory of our destiny, can really only be overcome by going into the Silence? By truly learning to hear and to listen through the heart, which integrates all lines of communication between one another, between ourselves and the natural world, between ourselves and our higher spiritual contacts, between ourselves and the stars and ultimately with Goddess-God? The five ears upon the stalk of wheat seem to indicate that this is so, as does the ancient Egyptian mystical teaching that the ears can open a secret doorway to the higher worlds – a secret doorway that we believe leads first to the 'nous', and thence to the apex of the pyramid, from where we can reach for the stars.

Wheat intolerance is endemic nowadays, especially in the West. Its consumption causes exhaustion and varying allergic reactions. This is a strange situation to arise concerning the ingestion of the Bread of Life, which is intended to bestow vitality and inner harmony. The Corn Maiden herself was transformed into the chalice of the Holy Grail in medieval art, signifying the life-giving and all-nourishing properties of the Grail. Could it be that our bodies and the natural world, which know about Mary Magdalene in the secret life of their cells and their primal consciousness relating to the origins of the earth and matter, are trying to wake us up to the truth, telling us that we are failing to digest it, or digesting it in the wrong way?

When the cords of communication which link us all are harmonized and integrated in the heart, the throat chakra expands and helps us to translate the love arising from the heart into compassion, tolerance, understanding and respect for the individual needs of others, which in turn inspires true union and steadfast brotherhood unassailed by the claims of the lower nature. The centre holds, and harmony, like the element ether, assumes a constant orbicular motion. That is why we might designate the spider as the animal connected with the throat chakra, for it is the creator and spinner of the etheric thread, its handiwork is designed always upon the principles of the mandala, and its home is the centre of the web.

When working with this chakra, meditate on the Silence (see Page 29) and the still, silent peace of the starry heavens. Ask your guardian angel to link you with the angels of order and harmony, and with the Angel of the Creative Word. You may find that this chakra (as well as the heart) is the particular centre your guardian angel uses to communicate with you. It will bless, gently awaken, and add its own essence to the seal that you apply to this chakra (the bright silver equal-sided cross in a circle of light), so that the delicacy and sensitivity of your throat chakra might be protected. It will stimulate and attune to the heart the holy light enshrined within it

Our guardian angel's message to us in helping us to rise to the challenges of the throat chakra might be given as: 'Listen; listen; listen; for you have been given ears to hear.'

The Brow Chakra

The sixth step of the pyramid is represented by the Third Eye, the brow chakra. It is linked with the planet Mercury, the messenger, and with the sixth sense. It also receives the influences of the planet Uranus. Its mystery is contained in the stars of the constellation Virgo and reflected in Gemini. Its colour is a perfect rose hue, like the first blush of sunrise. It is known as 'the abode of joy' and it is a centre of command, stimulating the divine light in every cell of the body in preparation for the ascension at the crown centre. It is associated with the single eye of Horus, and it is towards the Age of Horus (the New Age) that we are advancing. Mercury is connected with Horus because the mother of Horus, Isis, is synonymous with the Corn Maiden of Virgo, the zodiacal sign over which Mercury rules. With Uranus, Mercury's mission is to enlighten us through the brow chakra with sudden, sometimes shattering, illumination and revelation.

Intoxicated wisdom, or foolish wisdom, is the challenge of the sixth chakra. When the third eye remains closed to spiritual illumination and sees only earthly reality, it becomes filled with a sense of the rightness of its own opinions and adjusts reality according to its own illusions. While the third eye is focused on such illusion, then intuition and inspiration, the heavenly twins that bless the vision of the third eye and activate the sixth sense, are prevented from sporting and playing in the field of its vision. The result is intoxicated (in the sense of inebriation and toxicity), or foolish, wisdom. Mercury in his lower aspects can also turn intelligence into silver-tongued, self-serving cunning, manifesting as guileful wisdom.

The lesson of the brow chakra is to hone our consciousness to the point where 'the eye of the vision... in the soul' opens and commands the body and the five senses according to the new spiritual vistas opening up to its divine sight. Its job is to step up the vibration of physical reality and transform it from its mundane limitations into the limitlessness of the spirit. That is why the animal or creature of the sixth chakra is the hawk or the white eagle. Swift, high-flying and far-seeing, this bird is the divine messenger of the sun.

Ask your guardian angel to link you with the Angel of Creative Wisdom and the Angel of Discernment, and particularly with the angels of joy. Meditate with your angel on the Rainbow Bridge. This is the rainbow of natural phenomena, but it also extends from your brow centre (it is rooted in the heart) through your two crown centres, and out into the supernal heavens of the Imperishable Stars. You may also like to use The Candle of Vision meditation (and The Enchanted Fairy Isle meditation, given in Appendix III). Your guardian angel will walk with you over the bridge, and help you to garner an abundance of sacred light and inspiration from the celestial worlds. When you return together over the rainbow bridge, your angel will infuse your higher soul with this divine bounty.

Our guardian angel's message to us in helping us to rise to the challenges of the base chakra might be given as: 'Heed the message of the stars; for their message is in their beauty and in the lustral fires of their mystical radiance.'

The Crown Chakras

We now come to the seventh stair of the pyramid. This corresponds to the crown chakra, whose mystery is contained within the stars of the constellation Auriga, particularly the star Capella, 'Little Goat', which reflects the constellation of Capricorn.

If we think of the ecliptic, which is the annual path the sun seems to take around the earth and which represents the ring of the solar zodiac, we might imagine that this in itself is the crown chakra for the Soul of the World, the soul of all humanity. In my first book, *Earth Magic*, I wrote concerning this idea:

> There is a strange and beautiful night-time phenomenon, only occasionally to be seen in the northern hemisphere, called the Zodiacal Light. In springtime, it is just a glow in the western skies after the sun has set and gone. In the autumn, it can be seen in the east before sunrise, like a radiant mist with a pearly lustre set at its heart. But in the tropics its conical shape expands into a ring of light like a crown, some parts of it as brilliant as the stars.

> For those who believe that life has meaning, and that no phenomenon is senseless or random, this haunting light may seem to be a celebration of the zodiac itself, its stars and planets, the Sun and Moon which majestically tread its course, and the unending and unfathomable significance it has for our beloved Earth, the exquisite centre-jewel of the universe as we experience it.

The zodiac, both the ecliptic and the sidereal (the actual constellations themselves) can be viewed from this perspective as the earth's crowning glory.

The crown chakra of the individual human being is properly two centres, one at the top of the forehead at its midpoint, and one secreted in the middle of the brain. This shines from the crown on the scalp and is reflected in the Soul Star, the chakra above the top of the head, as our Earth Star is a reflection of the base chakra and exists below our feet, connected to our Vivaxis.

The kingly or queenly crown of jewels is a symbol of these topmost chakras and illumines their form and purpose, which is to receive the divine illumination of the stars and the supernal glory which shines behind their physical manifestation, and to give forth the light of Christ Consciousness so that the individual can take his or her place among the radiant stars.

When the chakras are fully developed and activated, the door which is the 'nous' opens like a great archway, and we become one with our divine spirit. When this happens, we do indeed become one of the great company of brilliant stars. We become independently radiant. This is the meaning of the eighth level of the pyramid, the apex above the base, which we reach by climbing the seven stairs – the ladder. Beyond the pinnacle are the starry heavens, our destiny and our destination.

Both of these chakras (the composite crown chakra) are associated with the moon, especially the one in the centre of the brain. Influences from Neptune and Mercury also govern these centres. Their colours are as a mystical rainbow, every combination of colours that we know on earth, and more beyond these. The one at the mid-point of the temples is where we attain cosmic consciousness. We become as 'the Woman Who Knows All'.

The chakra in the heart of the brain, which is a reflection of the 'nous', or the mind in the heart, and is so strongly linked with the full moon, is also closely connected with hearing and listening. It is a receiving and reflecting station which feeds the diadem whose central jewel is the point in the middle of the forehead between the temples, the flashing gem of divine wisdom. This full-moon chakra is like a lake reflecting the light of the spiritual star, which shines above the head. It becomes as the Sphere of John-Shar-On and is linked with the Pole Star.

Whilst ever we are unable to activate our chakras and pass through the 'nous' in full-moon consciousness, our being is like the moon we see from the earth – a beautiful shining entity which is gradually eaten by the darkness of the earth, but which is always reborn out of the belly of the night. It signifies the in-breath and the out-breath, the flowing and ebbing tide, sleeping and awakening and the process of reincarnation – being drawn back towards the earth.

When we attain our fully illumined state, however, the moon of our being remains imperishably full, just as we are one with the imperishable stars (the spiritual light of the celestial bodies). It is then that the chakra above our crown can be seen, pouring forth its effulgence in a starburst of rainbow colours, exquisitely radiant yet delicate, subtle, almost pearlized. The chakras take up the colours and each one spins in its own permutations of light, colour and sound, fabulous to behold.

The challenge of the crown chakra is self-righteous materialism, which manifests when a very narrow and bigoted sense of divinity is all that is allowed to develop, or when the ego mistakes itself for divinity, and pronounces its judgements (often only a reflection of its likes and dislikes and the restrictions of its viewpoint) as if on divine authority. Both of these states choke the motion of the chakras and cause their energies to stagnate.

The lesson of the crown chakra(s) is the attainment of cosmic consciousness through the development – in the heart – of love, wisdom and spiritual willpower (the will-to-good), which activate the chakras. The two animals connected with the two crown centres are the dragon (mid-brain) and the unicorn (mid-forehead). (Mary Magdalene and Jesus symbolize these chakras.)

Ask your guardian angel to connect you to the Mysterious Angel, the One who will bless us with cosmic consciousness and who serves Christ-Brigid, the Spirit and the Bride. This Great One is the overlighting angel of your own guardian angel, and of all guardian angels. It is linked with the identity of John the Beloved, who personified this mysterious angel of cosmic consciousness. Your angel will magnify and amplify your ability to safely receive his and her (for the Mysterious One comes with a consort) exalted consciousness into your chakras, and will stabilize it there. Meditate upon Silence. See it as a ring of pure and endless light, leading into the vastness of the starry heavens – not the starlit dome of the physical universe, but the stars that shine beyond the material stars, which are but a reflection of their glory. Ask your guardian angel to draw you close in spirit to the great Angel Sandalphon, and to help you to commune in spirit with him-her, according to your capacity.

Our guardian angel's message to us in helping us to rise to the challenges of the crown chakras might be given as: 'Watch with care and discernment every word you say; for you are the Utterer of the Word, and you hold the divine balance of the cosmos within your innermost heart.'

Some Points to Note

It is a common teaching in the West that the chakras correspond to the colours of the rainbow, from red (the base chakra) to violet at the crown. This is a misconception. No such rigid system applies. The chakras do reflect the colours of the rainbow, but in a multitude of varying hues, many of which we have never experienced on earth, and their source is the Soul Star, the Rainbow Seat, rather than the assignation of a colour by inherent design, although a system does loosely exist, taught by the Eastern mystics, as follows:

1 Never stimulate the chakras by mental concentration. They must be allowed to develop naturally, through spiritual aspiration, which is conscious attunement to the highest good.

2 You can open your chakras before commencing meditation by gently visualizing them spinning in a clockwise direction and emanating white light. Let your focus be soft and brief so that there is no danger of overcharging them.

3 Drugs and excessive alcohol, as well as extreme emotional states and some forms of medication, overcharge the chakras to a damaging extent.

Meditation will help to harmonize overcharged chakras. However, do not relinquish medication before seeking advice from a doctor.

4 Always seal your chakras after meditation or similar activity. Use the symbol of a circle of light containing a bright silver equal-sided cross, and imaginally place it over each chakra in turn, starting at the top (the crown).

—◌ A N G E L I C   S E E D - T H O U G H T S ◌—

When you are disturbed in your spirit, think of the
angel of peace.
When you need help to forgive and to understand,
open your heart to the angel of love;
let the angel of wisdom shine through your thoughts.
And on dark days, think of the angel of joy,
let the angel of joy bring sunshine
into your heart.

White Eagle

When Gilda,...the personification of the spirit of the
dance... walked or ran she hardly seemed to touch the
ground with her feet. She reminded me of a curious
fact which I have noticed, that most of us dash
through life, elbowing one another, jostling, bustling,
tripping and generally following a vertiginous
rhythmless course until Death ends the race. Some
there are who dance their way through life, following
an inexorable rhythm...

Walter Starkie, *Raggle-taggle*

CHAPTER SEVEN

STAR MAGIC

We have seen how purifying and activating the chakras through the heart-centre, with the help of our guardian angel, leads us to the summit of the pyramid of our being. When we enter our soul-temple in full consciousness, having overcome the unconsciousness or the 'sleep' of materialism that prevents the divine fire in our chakras from springing into full life, the ineffable light of the spirit floods our crystal castle (our soul-body), and we become contained in our tower of light, which manifests on the subtle planes as a radiantly golden pyramid. As this golden pyramid (our enlightened self) becomes entirely suffused with the illumination of the Godhead, we actually become a star, because the supernal consciousness also takes the form of a pyramid in which to enter us and fill us, only this pyramid is downward-pointing. It is the sacred V, the Holy Grail that carries the celestial consciousness down to earth from the spiritual realms. When the inverted pyramid interpenetrates the upward-pointing pyramid (ourselves united with our higher, spiritual nature), the star of our true self comes into being. Thus we are made ready to connect with the mystical energies of the starry heavens. It is our guardian angel's specially appointed task to help us with this great work – the true alchemical consummation.

All this wonder takes place at the 'eighth level', the very apex of our upward-pointing pyramid, which is our subtle and divine structure. The eighth level is the Bridal Chamber, where the Mystical or Sacred Marriage takes place; and the Bridal Chamber looks out onto the boundless stars. The eighth level creates an octave, a perfect unit of harmonious creation (see the preceding chapter), which has its resonance, not only in our base chakra at the bottom of the spine, but in our 'eighth chakra', the one that reflects the base chakra and is connected to our Vivaxis which I have outlined in Chapter Six. It seems that the accurate picture which is beginning to emerge is that the heart chakra is actually a double chakra, and, in fact, so is the base chakra.

The true glory of what this means is that the whole chakra structure connects us to the stars, and that we can bring the rarefied nature of the stars, their energy and consciousness which is miraculously contained in their radiance, right down into the earth, and into our hands and feet. We have to sacrifice our lower self, the self of earth which attaches us to matter, in order to achieve this. Surely this deeply mystical secret must be contained in the esoteric symbolism of the pierced hands and feet of the crucified Christ?

I have found, through working with my guardian angel on purifying the chakras, that there comes a natural inclination to open the heart and the crown centres to the starry heavens, to explore the mysteries and the loveliness of the essence of the stars with the heart and mind through the inspiration of my angel. This is an aspect of the magical nature of the relationship that develops between a guardian angel and its human charge. The guardian angel takes us into the heart of things, and begins to reveal the secrets of the stars to the open, wondering, childlike heart and mind that, in expressing such qualities, can receive the scintillating treasure that is poured into its vessels. These star-scatterings that we receive from our angel are intrinsic to its teachings, because the guardian angel mirrors and would awaken the beauty of our soul; and, in showing us how to unfold its mysteries, is itself our lodestar.

I would like to share with you this star magic. My guardian angel often leads me out under the stars, in actuality or in meditation. Occasionally I am guided to read a book or a poem, or listen to music, for the purpose of deepening the knowledge I receive, or, perhaps, more accurately, transcribing my angel's star-teachings into words. I have found that listening to music from our own mystical tradition, or one with which we feel profoundly in harmony (mine is Celtic mysticism) helps the star wisdom to translate itself into language.

You may like to follow suit, and allow your angel to lead you out under the stars, to receive and to remember. So that this quicksilver wisdom is not lost, note it down in a star journal. Reading it many times, particularly before you sleep, will exponentially unveil the meaning of the star lore you receive so that you can understand more deeply its many-splendoured facets; and it will remind you of the beautiful, peaceful times of communion that you have spent under the stars with your angel.

You can use the following guided visualization in connection with your spiritual journeys in starlight. It is concerned with the recognition of cosmic consciousness through awareness of the star people, the Kontombili, who move between dimensions. The continent of Africa has a special connection with our deepest origins, which actually lie out among the star fields; and with the great mystery of the stars themselves.

Spiritual teachers, seers and esotericists from numerous cultures speak of the god-people who came to earth in its very beginnings, when humanity was newborn. The wisdom of these teachers and seers tells us that our earth and its humanity is much older than our present calculations suggest, and that there is a spiritual reason for the existence of the relics which have been unearthed in our own time by palaeontologists. We can understand only dimly at present, but the suggestion is that a terrible cataclysm occurred, caused by human foolishness, that sank the two great continents of Atlantis and Mu (which were perhaps contiguous to one another, because Australian aboriginals speak of a 'great land break-up' that occurred in their unimaginably far past, although their elders still carry an inherited memory of the land-mass of the earth being divided into continents at that time). For a period of history after this world-shattering event, the spiritual dynamo which is evolution appeared to go into reverse before eventually balancing itself and moving forward once again. Evolution is a God-force, and so cannot actually decline or reverse; however, there was a need for the soul of humanity to retrace its steps, which gave rise to the appearance that the evolutionary forces temporarily travelled backwards.

Prior to this planetary disaster, humankind had evolved beautiful and enlightened civilizations, advanced beyond our wildest dreams. They had been built upon the mysteries revealed to them by the god-people, who came from the stars to instruct us, and in time left, leaving behind their legacy in temples and hidden centres which were guarded by the elders, highly evolved human souls who knew how to use and dispense their magnificent heritage with wisdom, balance and spiritual poise.

There were also on the earth at this time many young souls, who had known very few incarnations. They lived in great joy within these mighty civilizations, which were created by spiritual power to vivify the soul and to harmonize with the natural world. Unfortunately, the lower nature of these very young souls overcame them, and they stormed the mystery-centres and the temples, forcibly wresting the secrets of the sacred god-power from their rightful keepers. Not being ready to receive such knowledge, they then commenced to abuse it in many ways, swiftly building systems of miraculous but lethal technology, the worst of which was a substance that was more powerful and deadly than the atom bomb, which they used to destroy vast countries and populations within seconds. Their evil depredations caused a negative spiritual force to come into being which drew a massive satellite directly into the path of the earth. All was destroyed, and the womb of the sea took back all that had arisen from her. Just a small scattering of elders were left to set sail to the farthest shores of the earth, each bringing their crumb of enlightenment to enable humanity to start again.

What we see in the tribes of Africa and other so-called 'primitive' societies are the vestiges of these previous civilizations which were unconscionably more enlightened than the humanity of today. Their rituals and beliefs have seemed to men of 'culture' to be based on vulgar superstition, but this is not so. These so-called 'primitive peoples' have sacrificed material comfort to keep alive for the sake of their planetary brethren a number of cells of the old knowledge that was brought to earth from the stars, so that in time we may build again, as in former days, but this time with perhaps even greater wisdom, humanity and insight, similar civilizations of spiritual power and majesty to those which were ours in the past.

These wisdom keepers have always protected their knowledge from outsiders, but now, it seems, the young souls who were left on earth to try to regain their lost paradise have at last attained a degree of preparation and readiness to receive it. Sensing this, and realizing how disastrous it would be for the future of humanity if their precious cell of knowledge were allowed to die (its wisdom keepers are becoming fewer and fewer, due to the incursions of Western 'civilization'), a young man called Malidoma Patrice Somé of the West African Dagara people decided to break the age-old silence and disseminate African wisdom to the world. He wrote a book called *Of Water and the Spirit*, his own autobiography, in which he reveals many mysteries concerning the connection of humanity with the spiritual worlds. One of the most direct of these describes his friendship with the Kontombili, a tribe of star people from the inner worlds who are higher up the evolutionary ladder than present-day humanity.

Whilst writing his book, Malidoma was aware that he was doing something entirely unprecedented which would bring down condemnation on his head from his own people. He describes how he often wept in great distress as he pulled back the sacred enshrouding curtain, and yet could not stop his hand from writing.

For those Westerners whom he has introduced to the Kontombili, their experience is an absolutely real and moving one. Many have held the hand of one of these beings for several minutes so that the resistance of their narrowly intellectual cultural conditioning could at last melt away, its resistance overcome by simple reality.

Malidoma has explained that the Kontombili are not just to be found in Africa. They are everywhere, because they are a star people. My first encounter brought me an awareness of a presence and some very strange sounds in the house! Afterwards I was able to perceive the wisdom of these people, and the sense of wellbeing and peace that they impart to those they encounter.

Meeting the Kontombili

Sit quietly and comfortably, clearing your mind by taking several complete breaths. Straighten and relax your spine, using support if necessary. Focus gently on your heart-centre, gradually slow the pace of your breathing, and enter into stillness.

You are moving through a peaceful West African tribal village. The round houses with their conical roofs glow richly golden in the early evening sun. You are aware that their shapes are sacred as you pass them by.

Food is being prepared and eaten outdoors, whilst children and dogs sit at some distance from the domestic fires, a few already asleep. An aura of simplicity and grandeur emanates from the village, the people majestic in their repose. An atmosphere of community spirit and ancient lawfulness pervades the scene, as though the village were built on the site of a temple dedicated to the evocation of a wise and timeless deity.

The village is set upon a wide plain between the foot of a rugged mountain and a great encircling forest. It occurs to you that perhaps the protective temple of the village is indeed the mountain, for you sense that it is holy.

As you come to a cluster of straw granaries bathed in the mellow evening light, a tall, slender man steps out from among them, apparently a member of the tribe, except that there is about him an unearthly beauty of form and feature, and that his body throws off a brilliant black, almost indigo, incandescence which you feel as warmth on your skin.

You know that he is the Spirit of the Ancestors who forever walks this land which is the cradle of the human race, and that he will lead you to your greater destiny.

Leading down into the village and up the slopes of the mountain is a well-worn path. The Spirit of the Ancestors beckons to you to follow him along its trail.

You climb the mountain behind your spirit-guide,

enjoying the warm, aromatic air, spiced now with the cooler currents and sharper fragrances of the evening. The way does not seem steep, yet everywhere you look you see grand vistas of the incomparable wilderness of Africa, suffused in sky-pools of fluid golden light.

Your guide leads you to the entrance of a cave, hung with fern-fronds and flowering tree-creepers. From their depths a huge owl watches you unblinkingly. You feel that the yellow lanterns of its eyes are a signal that you are waited for within.

Enter the sacred cave with your spirit-guide.

The light is green and dim in here. The cave leads gently downwards into a beautiful circular hall where once, many thousands of years ago, a whirlpool existed. In the middle of the round hall there is a rock, hewn naturally by the ancient waters into the smooth shape of a rustic throne. Facing the throne is a group of mysterious stalagmites and stalactites which lead out of the hall and away down a broad, twisting corridor into the secret heart of the great mountain.

Your guide leads you to the central throne. You move forward to sit in it, but your guide, the Spirit of the Ancestors, signals to you that instead, you must kneel before it and lower your forehead onto the rocky dais from which it emerges.

You kneel together. You notice that the stone is warm, as though a mighty fire burned in the earth below the cave floor, like an inner sun.

You raise your head almost involuntarily, because you are aware that there is a presence in the hall, centred before you on the throne.

Your eyes fall upon the graceful contours of an immense black Goddess. She is seated upon the throne and yet she fills all the hall, the entire mountain and, it seems, even the skies beyond, for you are aware of the twinkling of stars and the turning of planets within the calm vastness of her body. You feel that she is Mother Africa, and also the Great Goddess Isis herself.

With a smile of infinite tenderness she smiles and draws you to her. 'You must recognize and absorb the black earth-energies before your quest can be fulfilled,' she says to you. Her voice is deep and rich as the booming hush of giant waves on some untrodden pacific shore.

Although you are as a miniscule atom within her measure-lessness, she takes your hands and looks into your eyes.

You suddenly feel that you are a bobbing ball upon the giant plume of a fountain of energy which rises up from the bowels of the earth and is yet sourced within the heart of the Goddess upon her throne. The magical black energies of the earth rise through you and set you dancing upon their ecstatic peaks.

You feel their power, their goodness, their healing and fecundity, their purity and sanctity, their wonder, their mystery, their beauty — the quintessence of the heart of the Great Mother Goddess. The knowledge comes to you that without these dark energies, so different from the darkness that humankind creates in its foolishness, there could be no springing life upon the earth and in the cosmos.

As your awareness of the energies recedes, the Goddess enters into intangibility, so that her presence still blesses the cave but you can no longer see her seated upon the rocky throne.

The Spirit of the Ancestors leads you forward to another natural outcrop of rock in the approximation of a shrine, which stands before the group of stalagmites and stalac-tites as they wind away, eerily beautiful, into the fastnesses of the mountain.

'I will leave you here,' he says to you. 'It has been granted to you to meet with the People of Knowledge.'

He does not disappear, but is suddenly not there. You are alone in the cave.

You begin to notice a darting, flashing motion beyond the stalagmites, and the appearance of eyes shining in the darkness. Then twelve little human-like creatures, less than two feet tall, gather before you. They are dark-skinned, with West African racial features and long hair, touched with a suggestion of fox-red. Their eyes sparkle and their smile is enigmatic and warm-hearted, dancing with a wise humour.

You find that your communication with them is tele-pathic. They tell you that they are the Kontombili, that you have come here in quest of the magic of star peace, and that they will impart their knowledge of star peace to you as a gift.

They lead you to the centre of the cave and indicate to you that you should sit on the throne of rock. You are uncertain, but the Kontombili reassure you that this time it is right for you to do so. 'You are ascending to your higher self,' they tell you.

Take your seat upon the throne, and feel the solid caress of the rock as it supports your body. It is easy to sit relaxed and upright in this strange stone chair. Your deeper self, your enlightened self, comes fully into being as you take your first breath upon the chair; and you know that this is because you have found the sacred point of peace within, and that your consciousness was escorted there by the beautiful integrating Goddess-energies which eternally play around the stone seat.

The Kontombili form a ring around you. Within their circle you feel protected from the emanations of the mundane world. A deep calm descends on you; your irenic self, your spirit, unfurls its wings.

In the quietude of this moment, ask these questions:

'How can I find star peace within amidst the pressures and the pace of my everyday life?'

Listen with your inner senses to the answers they give you.

'How can I give star peace to all the troubles and anxieties of my psyche?'

Listen again within your own being for their response.

'What can I do to promote and nurture star peace within my own environment, and within the community in which I live?'

Let the Kontombili speak once more to your inner ear.

As your time together comes to an end, thank these ancient supernatural people for their gifts of wisdom. Know that you can consult them whenever you take the time to withdraw into the quiet of meditation, into the secret chambers of your soul.

The Kontombili begin to fade into the recesses of the cave. As they take their leave of you, the last to slip away into the shadows says to you, 'The state of peace is that which fills you when you walk in the presence of Divine Spirit; when you are separated from this Great Spirit, then confusion, imbalance, distress, fear, pain and anger can cause war to rage on the inner and the outer planes.'

You contemplate these words as you continue to sit alone on the rocky seat at the heart of the cave. As you do so, you begin to feel a benign presence at your side.

It is that of a great master dwelling in the spiritual worlds. He is dressed like a mighty tribal chief in the full regalia of his office, yet his eyes are kindly, and his demeanour, though noble, is gentle and caring.

You realize that the Kontombili have led you to this master on the inner planes, and that the route indicated by their teachings will always lead you to the feet of your own master.

The master who now stands beside you guides you safely home with a fatherly air, and imparts some simple affirmations to you so that you may begin to embrace the philosophy of star peace espoused by the Kontombili.

Return to normal consciousness, seal your chakras with

the bright silver cross in a circle of light, and give forth your affirmations, which these words may echo:

I choose peace.

I reject anger, chaos, violence.

I choose peace.

I reject impatience, cruelty, lack of faith.

I choose peace.

The Milky Way

Even when the air is lucid and the heavens are clear enough to reveal a beautiful spangling of stars, the sight of the Milky Way ineluctably draws the eye and awes the imagination. This 'Torrent of light and river of the air', as the poet Longfellow describes it, has been given numerous names by the people of the earth, and this nomenclature in itself hints at its secrets. The Hindus call it the 'Dove of Paradise' and the 'Court of God', and also 'The Path of Ahriman', for Ahriman is the Soul Stealer, who would walk this path if he could, claiming every star and every fibre of this 'delicate tossed veil of a dancing girl swaying against the wind' along the way.

Ahriman is the 'devil' of the earth element, whose ice-cold breath withers and destroys the life of the soul. Ahriman imposes his dominion by throwing the pall of his deathly vision over our perception of reality, so that we think we can measure it only by material calculation. He wants to limit the winged and free-ranging soul to the constrictions of the physical realm. 'Let us be realistic', he says, because he does not want us to pass beyond the limitations of his own sphere. He would rather imprison us there, and claim elemental overlordship. He has many prophets today, who sound his doctrine and spread his word.

When you feel heavy in spirits and weary of life, Ahriman is whispering to you. He is the darkener of the stars. Oust him by looking up to the Milky Way! There you will see the divine picture of your soul, ever young, ever lovely, ever present in the heavens, composed of stars and star-mists, the Wedding Garment itself! 'What

amplitude of space, what infinite depths it reveals, and how mysterious that filmy stardrift', says Fiona Macleod, the Celtic mystic, in
praise of the Milky Way and all that it means. It is the Milk of Brigid
the Radiant, the milk of human kindness, the milk from the Pure
Mother that alone will nourish our soul, for anything that acts
against the law of kindness does harm to the soul and dims its light.

The ancient Celts knew that Brigid was the guardian of the
white foaming milk, and the divine source of that spiritual principle
whereby milk manifests on earth through the mother. She was seen
as the symbol of giving, the holy dun cow that led pilgrims home
along the Milky Way to the Realm of the Imperishable Stars, deni-
grated nowadays, as the emblems of the sacred Feminine have been
for so long.

The people of the Scottish isles (the Hebrides) call the Milky
Way 'Arianrod' or 'the Silver Road', almost the name of the
Spinning Goddess of the Soul herself, aloft in her revolving tower or
castle of purest crystal; and, as must be so if our soul clothes our
chakras, and the chakras lead to the Bridal Chamber which looks
out onto the boundless stars, and where we ourselves become a star,
Ahrianrhad is Goddess of the Rising Stars.

The Hebridean islanders also call it 'the Road of the Kings' and
'the Pathway of the Secret People' (the initiates who have gained
soul-freedom, and the angels and spirits who aid them and light
their way). This is interesting, because one of the English names
for the Milky Way is 'Watling Street'. In our understated and prosaic
way, the English hide a Tookish secret beneath a Baggins-esque title!
It is derived from the Anglo-Saxon *Waetlinga Straet*, 'the Path of
the Waetlings', which refers to the giant sons of the mighty King
Waetla, who set out along their soul-path to achieve mythical deeds,
traversing earth and sea and heaven itself in their vast epic wander-
ings in search of that fabulous treasure – consummation with the
fully enlightened Soul in the glory of the Bridal Chamber or
Temple. So the name 'Watling Street' has the same measure of
heroic splendour as the Gaelic 'Road of the kings' and the
Scandinavian 'Woden's Way' or 'the Heroes' Way'.

When we attain soul-enlightenment, we do indeed attain the

glorious stature of our full manhood or womanhood. As Mary Magdalene says in her gospel, we become 'fully human'. The task is the span of all our lives, as the deeds of the heroes and the cosmic dimensions of the Milky Way confirm. And yet we are advised that we must never think of soul-enlightenment, or soul-ascension whilst still on earth, as a faraway, remote possibility, open to us only in some distant futurity. The time can always be now!

The essential femininity of the soul is also revealed throughout much of the nomenclature of the Milky Way. That title in itself was ancient in England in Chaucer's time, and has since spread over the globe (perhaps because of Milton's verse, which, in paraphrasing Ovid, names it as such '...that milky way/Which nightly as a circling zone thou seest/Powdered with stars...'), the reference in it attesting to the worship of Brigid in England as well as the more typically Celtic countries. Not only is it cited as the 'Path of the Dun Cow' in Britain, but it is named as 'the women's street' in Holland; and in England it is called 'Walsyngham Way' after the Virgin Mary, commonly referred to until the middle of the sixteenth century as 'Our Lady of Walsyngham' because her chief shrine in the country was located at Walsingham Abbey in Norfolk. This is interesting, as it designates the Milky Way as the sacred road to the 'virgin' in the starry heavens – the 'virgin' who is in actuality our own chakra-enlightened soul assuming the form of a star.

The soul associations go on and on. The Native Americans called it 'the Trail to Ponemah [the Hereafter]', and peoples as diverse as the Eskimos and the Bushmen of South Africa called it 'the Ashen Path', or the road of fire-ember signals, their smoking pyres put in place to lead the newly-arisen souls or 'ghosts' home.

Perhaps the most beautiful name for this great serpent of stars is the old Finnish one, Linnunrata, 'the Birds' Way'. It is called the 'Great Snake' in many traditions, and 'the Crooked Serpent' in the Book of Job, denoting the fiery serpent of the kundalini as it coils its way upwards from the base chakra to the crown chakra, and, in so doing, irradiates the soul in a great starburst of light. This designation arises from a time-honoured Estonian belief, with its roots in the knowledge of the ancient world, that once, by a miracle, all the songs of all the birds of the earth were turned into a cloud of tiny snow-white wings and ranged across the heavens as a divine road from heaven to the 'high places' of the earth.

From what we know of the mystical link between angels and birds, we can read a sublime message in the ancient Gaelic names for the Milky Way of 'Court of the Angels' and 'the Kyle of the Angels', 'kyle' meaning 'sound'. In other words, the Milky way is the Court of the Angels, which is synonymously the 'sound' of the angels, itself a bridge created by the divine act of gathering together all the birdsong in the world and setting it as a 'mystical link' between the high places of the earth (raised consciousness or conscious human communion with angels) and heaven.

These are the secrets of the Milky Way; that it is a manifestation of the mystery of the soul, the Wedding Garment of the eternal spirit; that its lights and star clusters and fire-mists are symbols of the wonders and beauties and jewels of the soul, waiting to manifest as we unfold it and purify its chakras; that it represents the interplay between birds and angels, and promises us their commingling qualities of song, flight, spiritual beauty, freedom and a rapture beyond imagining; that it is the road to royalty in the real sense of the word, which designates each one of us as true sons and daughters of the King and the Queen (Father-Mother God); and that it stands surety that each one of us will become a star, emitting our own light, and that we will pass into the Realm of the Imperishable Stars, the Land of the Ever Young, the Sphere of the Blest. Contemplate these things with your guardian angel; sit with it out under the stars of the Milky Way, the Linnunrata, (which even sounds rather like a phrase of beautiful birdsong in itself!), and gaze in peace at this Court of Angels. You will receive truths and splendours from its endless store for yourself, truths not cited here, because they are yours.

If you feel that these things sound very fine and pleasing, and uplifting to think about, but could never really be true in the scheme of things as it appears to exist from the earthly point of view, or if there is an Ahrimanic pull within you, advising you that such beliefs are rather silly, consider this: every law upon the earth, every truth as it reveals itself to you, every step you take upon the way in company with your angel and your guide, will confirm these things to you more and more clearly, more and more profoundly, more and more ringingly, until you will at last begin to live in the light of the joy of this knowledge. It is the wonder that the stars proclaim.

Never forget that the guardian angel tirelessly brings to us opportunities for spiritual unfoldment, and lovingly and devotedly cleanses the jewels of our spirit – all its unique, individual gifts – so that they radiate through the soul. This is how the soul builds its celestial temple, which is constructed throughout many, many lives so that it might clothe the spirit, the divine spark or seed-atom of mystic light which is the Child of God within our hearts. There are two aspects to the soul. One is the greater Soul, which spins and weaves and builds as it receives (and enters and blesses) worthwhile material from human experiences on earth. The other is the 'lesser' soul, the inner essence of the everyday self confined to the present life, and is actually a little strand of the greater Soul, a hand mirror of it which reflects its pristine light and can garner into its mirroring substance those qualities which enlighten and quicken the soul (both aspects of it, lesser and greater) as we live our everyday lives.

Our guardian angel's great task is to strengthen and nurture the line of light (magically linked to the spine and the chakras) which joins us to our Higher Self (our greater soul and our spirit) in the heavenly realms. Our guardian angel is connected to the great Recording Angel (our ability to record sounds and images is an emanation of this being) and records every minute detail of our life. These records create our karma, positive and negative, which has to be balanced. Our guardian angel brings us karmic opportunities to repay debts and so restore balance and harmony.

The heart is the altar where we link with our guardian angel, and our other angel helpers. After making the link with our heart, the guardian angel and our angel group also make use of other chakras to link with us in communion, particularly the throat centre.

When we look out upon the great Milky Way, our own beloved galaxy which shows us, as a miracle, the structure of our own individual soul, we can ponder these things, and, perhaps, remember particularly that its name is also, in the Hebridean isles, 'the Pathway of Peace'. Meditation on the Milky Way, on the Wedding Garment with all its muted glittering and soft brilliance, imparts a peace borne to us by angels.

Fiona Macleod, through her meditation on the Pathway of Peace, was given the following insight – again, it emphasizes the soul, for the bodies of water on the earth are deeply symbolic of it.

> Last night I watched the immense tract for a long time. There was frost in the air, for I saw that singular pulsation which rightly or wrongly is commonly held to be an optical illusion, the aspect as of a pulse, or of an undulating motion of life such as one might dimly perceive in the still respiration of some sleeping saurian. There appeared to be countless small stars, and in the darker spaces the pale vaporous drift became like the trail of phosphorescence in the wake of a vessel: at times it seemed almost solid, a road paven with diamonds and the dust of precious stones, with flakes as of the fallen plumage of wings – truly Arianrod, the Silver Road, as the Celts of old called it. Of course it was no more than a fantasy of the dreaming imagination, but it seemed to me more than once that as a vast indefinite sigh came from the windless but nevertheless troubled sea, there was a corresponding motion in that white mysterious Milky Way, so infinitely remote. It was as though the Great Snake – as so many bygone peoples called and as many submerged races still call the Galaxy – lay watching from its eternal lair that other Serpent of Ocean which girdles the rolling orb of our onward-rushing earth: and breathed in slow mysterious response: and, mayhap, sighed also into the unscanned void a sigh infinitely more vast, a sigh that would reach remote planets and fade along the gulfs of incalculable shores.

Fiona Macleod, *Where the Forest Murmurs*, 1906

Fiona Macleod, with all her beautifully attuned subtle and mystic senses, seems to have witnessed in her meditations on the Milky Way a perfect expression of the old mystery school teaching: 'As above, so below.'

CHAPTER EIGHT

THE SEVEN LAMPS
OF HEAVEN

If the Milky Way is a reflection of the Wedding Garment (the soul), and our own individual souls in turn reflect this wonder of the heavens, there must be seven heavenly lamps – stars or star-groups – that have a macrocosmic association with our individual chakra system. We know that the stars of the zodiac, and the planets of our solar system, are linked via their influences with our chakras, and that they provide us with lessons, challenges and revelations that guide us along our personal life-path. But are there other, subtler and yet more universal star influences?

It seems that there are, although they affect only the higher chakras, with the exception of the first (base) chakra, because there is a sense in which the first step up the pyramid (the base chakra represents this first step) contains all the others within it. This is the purpose of life on earth – to ascend in spirit so beautifully and per- fectly that we actually spiritualize the earth (the base chakra) and take it with us to the highest heights. Within the base chakra lies hidden the secret of the eighth chakra and its mysterious Vivaxis energies, which is also affected by these higher star influences. The two chakras which, it seems, are not responsive to them are the sacral and the solar plexus chakras, the centres of our 'feminine' and 'masculine' desire nature, the sacral chakra being the feminine, inwardly-inclined centre of desire ruled by water and the moon, and the solar plexus chakra the outwardly-inclined centre of desire ruled by fire and the sun, although because the fires of desire are reflected, astral fires and not the true flame of spirit, the element of the solar plexus chakra is air, not fire (see Chapter Six).

These solar and lunar desire centres are connected with the lower aspects of the sun and the moon (meaning the way in which our earthly nature responds to the sun and moon influences), and so they cannot directly receive the high-frequency spiritual emanations from the stars, the 'seven lamps of heaven' which are sending beautiful impulses down to our earth so that we might absorb them into our consciousness. They receive their baptism of purifying light and become virginal through the action on them of the base and the higher chakras, when these are so in attunement that the fire of the kundalini rises to the crown, and beyond into the starry heavens of the spiritual realms. An ancient example of nomenclature for the seven main chakras is 'the Seven Virgins of Light', perhaps confirming my belief that the true understanding of a 'virgin' is one who is secure within their crystal tower of light created by the immaculate radiance of their purified chakras – the soul perfected.

Therefore, although the 'seven lamps of heaven' equate to the chakras, they affect only the base and Vivaxis chakras, the heart chakra, the throat chakra, the brow chakra, and the two crown chakras. We can contemplate such information, and then leave technicality aside as we go out as in ritual under the stars, to receive their joy and blessing in company with our guardian angel. We do not have to worry about which chakra equates to which star! Our angels and guides, and the great Star Beings, will do all that is needful. Our task is simply to open our heart – our higher consciousness – to the stars.

Arcturus

The star, Arcturus, sends us the scintillating energy of hope. It works with our heart chakra to gently clear away all the heaviness, the sadness, the fear and anxiety, the gloom and despondency which darken the vision and cause hopelessness, and which are especially associated with the oppressions of the soul arising from our base chakra. Through the heart, Arcturus blesses this chakra, and our eighth chakra connected to our Vivaxis energies. It has a beautiful grounding quality, and magically stabilizes and balances our soul-light (flowing from our spirit) so that we can draw up the ancient spiritual light locked into the earth (just as our own light is locked into our base chakra) and give it forth in healing through our hands and our feet. Let our feet bless the earth. Let our hands bless others, and our own lives.

The Arcturian seeds of hope come to flower and fruition in our responsiveness, in our firm resolve not to resist and deny the dancing spirit of hope. Ahriman, the darkener of the stars, will at some point press in upon you as you extend your hand to this joyous spirit, urging you to manifest sad wraiths of doom and despondency. Gently release these into the care of your guardian angel, and call on your angel to water and irradiate the seeds of hope that Arcturus has sown in your heart. Your emotional self will become buoyant and free, your body will feel lighter, your mind stable, swift and expansive.

The sweet hope that Arcturus brings to us clears negative energies. Wherever there lurk stagnant, brooding frequencies, the Arcturian emanations will sweep away the illusion and freshen the spiritual air currents. It blends the evolution of the human family with the evolution of the Earth herself, connecting the Earth's beautiful heart chakra with our own. It carries the Earth's heart-light out into her grid system, circulating her blood and healing blockages. Mother Earth's grid system is incomplete, and needs our healing. Only then can we ourselves be truly healed. By absorbing energy from the stars and treading softly and mindfully (connecting our mind with our heart) upon the earth with loving footfalls, we can help to renew and replenish our beloved planet, who has become starved of certain frequencies due to our abuse and misuse of the cosmic powers.

Arcturian frequencies are imbued with the finer essence of water. They are very ancient, and have facilitated our cellular evolution since the beginning of life on earth. They fall as a soft ethereal shower of renewing, pearlized rain upon the earth, and upon our souls. We can receive them into ourselves by imagining this sublime shower of subtle pearly raindrops falling into our deepest heart, and gently streaming through our auric field, as we stand beneath the stars to commune with Arcturus. See your heart chakra and your base chakra as connected, pulsing with spiritual light as you give yourself to the subtle influences of this magical rainfall from the stars.

Receive the earth energies from your Vivaxis, into your left foot at the centre, up your left leg to the centre of your left hand, where they then cross over between your heart and solar plexus centres, travel down your inside right leg, enter your right foot at the centre, travel back up the outside right leg, and into your right hand at the centre, at which point they leave your body and return to the Vivaxis. See these energies performing this ever-streaming, centring rite for a moment, remembering that you are never without your Vivaxis energies because there is a constant circulating flow back and forth from your Vivaxis. Then let the beautiful Arcturian emanations rain down into the Vivaxis flow, entering it and circulating through and with it. Feel the blessing in your hands and feet. Ask your guardian angel to stabilize it there, so that it is an ever-replenishing source for you to draw on. Thank your angel, and the Arcturians, who are a considerably ancient civilization, unconscionably more advanced than our own.

Know that you now hold the great clearing dynamics of Arcturus in your hands and feet centres, your eighth chakra connected to your Vivaxis, and in your base and heart chakras. Therein, the sweet fountain of hope springs eternally, never to run dry. If circumstances occur in your life or the balance of your subtle bodies to cast a dark veil over this clear wellspring of hope, connect with your guardian angel, and, working with your angel, summon the Arcturian stream, from above, from below, with your hands open and your feet spread and receptive, to receive its divine, freeing inrush. Let your heart, your consciousness, and your guardian angel balance and harmonize the flow with your receptive vessels until you feel restored. This harmony will integrate the dynamics of your conscious and unconscious mind, give life and vivid being to your dreams so that you can draw wisdom from them, and gently irradiate the energies of the moon as they work within your subtle centres.

Remember, the moon rules your sacral chakra, the female-attuned desire body; but it is also the great symbol of the soul-temple

that you are building throughout your lives on earth. It is your
mother, building and perfecting the temple, the body, of which you
will one day take full possession, to become a divine being whose
essence is an imperishable star – and the Arcturian energies come to
us on the universal Mother emanation.

This beautiful Arcturian connection with water reminds us that
the red colour of the base chakra, rich as a cavern of flawless, irradiated rubies, is the colour of our blood, and of universal love. Arcturus
has a strong connection with our blood, and of its dispensation, from
and through the heart, of the universal life force, which is love. Our
cellular water is a sublime liquid crystal that can hold and transcribe
ever higher and more subtle energy frequencies, the essence of divine
fire, God-touched consciousness. The blood comes under the influences of the Second Ray of creation, the Love-Wisdom Ray, upon
which Arcturus works. At the moment, we as a planetary civilization only express the lower vibrational frequencies of the love-energy
carried by the blood. We often seem able only to love those of 'our
blood', whether family, tribe or country, and only able to express the
blood's Fourth Ray influence (Harmony, especially harmony through
the balancing of dualities), as love of conflict, rather than love of
harmony through reconciliation of opposites!

The Arcturian influence will help us to step up the frequencies
carried by our blood, so that we truly begin to express all-embracing,
unconditional love for one another, and for all the kingdoms of our
planet. Esoteric teachers have spoken of a highly significant triangle
of subtle energy that is moving between the heart chakra of the sun,
the heart chakra of the earth, and the heart chakra of Arcturus.
This mighty spiritual structure connecting these three mystical
hearts is acting like a pyramid, which absorbs and stabilizes the
heart-energies and frequencies of higher consciousness, and then
sends these exquisite pulsating waves of divinity down into the
earth's base chakra, so that she may hold and store them, and merge
her consciousness with them, ultimately, to give to us, her children.

All is done from the heart, the heart which is love, which is
balance. The heart emanates love and connects with the base
chakra, the base chakra extends the 'Everlasting Arms' of love

'underneath' (at the base) of all that is, which, for us as we understand it from our perspective, is our Mother Earth. The arms are
extended by the hands, and the hands contain divine centres of
consciousness at their centre (emanations of the eighth chakra)
which connect to the heart of all things. 'Underneath are the
Everlasting Arms.' This is no sentimental saying; it is cosmic exac-
titude! How protected we may feel through the agency of these
Arcturus influences, and how secure in our hope!

There is an old story that seems to tell of this great moving
pyramid between the sun's heart, the earth's heart, and Arcturus. It
is said that the mighty Finn, King of the West, went hunting with
his hounds and his spears. He came upon a great bear, and chased it
to the ends of the earth, to the North Pole itself. The bear penetrated deep into the ice mountains of the Pole, and came upon the
sacred place where there is an everlasting rainbow. It climbed the
rainbow, meaning to escape to the opposite polarity of the earth; but
Finn sent his hounds to pursue it, and at last brought it down in a
rain of shining spears. Thinking the beast must be dead, he
approached it; but the bear got up on its feet and prepared to flee
again, whereupon Finn continued to impale it with spears. God was
merciful to the bear, and caught her up into the shining black deeps
of the Arctic sky. Finn's hounds hung onto its tail, and so were
carried skywards too. Finn took the hero's leap, and with one jump
was on the Pole, and with the next was in the Northman's Torch
(Arcturus), and with the third was on the Hill of Heaven itself,
where he remains still.

I would interpret this myth as a mortal king's efforts to capture
and claim the elusive quarry of perfect kingship, which, in its greater
sense, is associated with the perfected soul-state where the elements
can no longer claim dominion over the soul, because the purified
chakras fortify it against the lower or outside influences, and in the
divine Bridal Chamber it has become a star and assumed its
'kingship'. Finn nearly manages it, sending his 'hounds' (his will
and desire) after his prey up the sacred chakra trail of the rainbow.
But he tries to storm the Bridal Chamber, or assume kingship, by
force. The bear is lifted into the heavens as an unattained ideal,

although his desire and his will still cling to it. Finn, realizing that there must be self-sacrifice, not coercion by arms, takes the 'hero's leap' onto the Pole (he aligns himself with the earth's heart chakra), from there to Arcturus (who endows him with hope, and further opens his own heart chakra in resonance with that of the earth), and from there leaps into the heart chakra of the sun (the 'Hill of Heaven itself'), where he becomes a 'fixed' or imperishable star.

From this legend, we can see that the great pyramid that moves between the heart chakras of the earth, Arcturus, and the sun (Divine Spirit), although imbued with a cosmic mission, is performing a like task for every single individual soul on earth – endowing us with an enhanced and increased opportunity to claim kingship, or soul-perfection. The association of King Arthur with the Great Bear, which Finn pursues and which is, of course, the polar constellation of the Great Bear with its seven clarion-bright stars, is ancient, and precedes the chieftan who became King Arthur at the end of the fifth century AD. Legend has always spoken, myth has always hinted, at a remote, celestial Arthur, a mighty warrior of light from the stars, true-hearted and God-smitten, of the essence of the spiritual sun, the protective spirit of the Grail or heart chakra of the world, which is Britain herself. Half-angel, half-God, he descends to earth from the region of the stars.

Folk tales say that the earthly King Arthur had a dream before he assumed his kingship; and in that dream he was taken up into the constellation of the Great Bear, where he found himself with seven mighty, supernal kings, lords of creation. The greatest of these stood, and addressed him, along with the heavenly company, thus: 'Comrades in God,' he said, 'the time is come when that which is great shall become small.' On saying this, the great king became a star, and the company six further stars; and Arthur fell from the skies as a meteor, as though the great king, and all the assembly, had passed their essence into him. The Little Bear constellation opposite that of the Great Bear is there, says the inspiration of fairy-tale and dreams, to show us this process – how the great one became small, and came to earth in human guise. As he approached the earth, he became a cloud (clothed in astral matter), and then a wisp of mist, which touched the earth (his greater spirit entered the Sphere of Illusion, the watery substance that hides the sun, as the earth is known to the sages).

Thereafter began his renowned kingship, upon the instigation of which he chose 'seven virgin knights' from the court of his father, King Uther Pendragon, to show the world the way of true kingship, and how to attain it for ourselves, and all the earth. And as the earth's saviour he became known, for it is said that Arthur never died, but only sleeps, and that he will come again to deliver the Earth and her peoples from suffering and darkness. He took the shape of a bear, because it is an emblem of the clothing and shape of the earth (the element of earth and the bear have always been synonymous), but also to show us that he did not come alone. In countless legends, from Greece, to North America, to China, the Great Bear of the constellation has ever been cited as feminine. He came in the company of one just as illustrious, just as star-strewn in spirit, who was yet hidden. She was his true consort, his magnificent queen; and if the sleep of earth had not hidden her true significance and obscured from his recognition the radiance his heart held for her, Camelot, the New Jerusalem, would have been grounded unfadingly into the earth, and the Seven Candlesticks of St John's Revelation would have illumined the human family forevermore. Instead, he chose the False Bride, Guinevere, the Wandering One (a translation of 'Guinevere'), which shows that she was as a planet, not yet illumined, not yet a star (the planets wander, the stars are fixed, in their courses) as he was, and therefore not a fitting queen. And so the Reign of Arthur, or Arth Uthyr (Arth means bear, Uthyr, great or wondrous one) was doomed to blow away into the sands of time, like all other reigns – until he comes again, this time in full consciousness of, and hand in hand with, his true beloved, when at last we shall all be made free.

Such are the mysteries of Arcturus, so connected with Arthur's name. With Arthur (Arcturus), with the sun, with the earth, all moving in harmony with the mysterious pyramid that links them, and thus in heart-alignment, shall come the dawn of the new day – and its name is Hope.

Find Arcturus by locating the Great Bear (the Plough) in the heavens, and following the direction in which the handle of the Plough points across the skies until you spot a large, bright star more or less in line with it. Arcturus is in the constellation of Boötes, and is the fourth brightest star in the heavens. It is a giant star and its colour is rich yellow. It doesn't matter if you are not sure where it is – you can still receive its energies!

Polaris

The beautiful North Star, our Pole Star, also shines in every human heart. It is our birthright and our gift, and, if we so wished (one day we must, if we are to survive as a planetary civilization) we could call upon its wondrous spectrum of healing, nourishing, protective, revivifying and inspiring powers throughout every moment of our lives.

The Pole Star shines in our hearts, upon our brow, and above us in the skies. It is the deeper essence of each one of us. It is our source, it is enlightened consciousness, and the destiny towards which we journey.

Once, inconceivably long ago, the Polaris continent was in existence around the North Pole, which was genial and temperate in climate in those far-off days. This was the legendary Garden of Eden, inhabited by god-men and goddess-women, who taught newborn humanity the art and the craft of living. Humanity was gradually overwhelmed by its own lower nature, and it fell from grace, out into the stark, unforgiving realm of deepest matter that we inhabit today.

The message of the Pole Star to us is that we will regain that lost paradise if we will only follow the star in our heart, which some call the Christ essence. It is the flame of God, the gift of the Mother and the Father. It is universally recognized by esotericists as the Divine Child, the Son-Daughter. We know it as the star in the heart, and it shines at our centre, above our heads, and all around us, for we exist at its heart. It is six-pointed, and has no inner divisions. We find it via the breath, directing the breath 'through the heart' until we are suffused with the peace that arises from that still, shining star and its brightly shining light, which is of an angelic essence, although its life is instinct with a fire that reaches beyond even the angelic realms.

The North Star has been given many names which are deeply reminiscent of its mystery. It is called Septentrion, for its magic contains the seven rays of creation. It has been known as the Gate of Heaven, the Lodestar, the Star of the Sea. In the Far East, it is the Imperial Ruler of Heaven, and in the Near East, it is called the Torch of Prayer, forever burning at the portal of the celestial Mecca – another 'Gate of Heaven'. Fiona Macleod, listening to an ancient and poignantly beautiful ballad about the North Star, sung to her by an old woman of the Scottish isles, remembers that it was referred to as 'the House of Dreams'. Northern cultures have honoured it with titles such as the Throne of the Gods, the Seat of the Mighty, the Portal of the Unknown. The Norsemen saw in it the abode of Heimdallr, the guardian of the rainbow which unites heaven and earth, and, from our microcosmic point of view, the star in the heart is indeed the sacred guardian of the chakras, the divine abode of the light which alone can safely summon the light locked so securely in the base chakra (or the earth) to the Bridal Chamber beyond the chakras, so ensuring that the rainbow bridge does not become dislocated and defiled.

Much of its nomenclature associates the Pole Star with God's Holy Mountain. It is Albordy, 'the dazzling mountain on which was held the Assembly of the Gods' of the ancient Teutonic peoples, the mysterious Mount Mêru, the seat of the gods of Aryan mythologers, whilst the Hindu sages referred to it as 'the holy mountain of God', which is also alluded to in Ezekiel. In the West, it is known as the Lamp of the North.

According to spiritual teachers, the North Star blesses us with a special magic which empowers us to work with our breath, so that we may become masters of 'inspired respiration' – breathing the breath of God. We do this by breathing through the heart. Sit or stand under the stars, and ask your guardian angel to breath with you, and to help you direct your breathing 'through your heart' in the way that is easiest and most harmonious for you. Ask your angel to pray with you to the Star of the North for this magical blessing of breath. This act of 'star breathing' facilitates the development and expression of our Christ consciousness. It gives us the dynamic of what might be called 'the peaceful will' – a steadfast, centred, grounded willpower which works gently and peacefully throughout every aspect of our life, without coercion or aggression. Thus may we beautifully fulfil the plan that was laid out for us from the beginning, and harmoniously weave the intricate and lovely designs that are uniquely ours into the web whose strands connect our higher nature with its earthly expression, without our rhythm being constantly broken by interference from those aspects of ourselves which block, hamper and emasculate the power of the higher will. Polaris, through the star in the heart, unites our heart-consciousness with our mental consciousness, so that the two become one and shine like a radiant jewel at the brow centre. This is done through our heart-attuned breath; when we breathe in heart-attunement, our breathing helps Mother Earth herself to breathe, and, through the resultant starry circulation of her breath, to be healed.

The Pole Star is associated with the Sphere of John or the Orbit of Sharon, which is a spiritual realm of peace, beauty and wisdom promised to the Earth and her peoples, and which will eventually descend as the 'new Jerusalem', once we have made proper preparation for its descent. The Pole Star is a double star, and we might think of one of its spheres as represented by the Jesus energy in the heart (the star), and the other as the Mary Magdalene energy in the heart, which manifests as the rose, and is the 'heart of hearts' of the star. Of course, this is a somewhat crude reduction of a sublime truth, because the star and the rose are of one essence; but there is a certain correct understanding in it, as long as we remember that the divine vessel which is the heart, which is the Christ, and which was the perfect attunement of Mary Magdalene and Jesus when they walked the earth as the immaculate expression of that divine vessel, is always one. Breathe in its spiritual starlight – breathe it out to heal the world.

Polaris is to be found by locating the two stars that form the top of the square of the Plough (the top two stars being those furthest

away from the handle). These are called the 'Pointers', and they
form a line pointing across the sky to a northerly, bright star, which
is Polaris. One of its twin stars shines with a subtle, heavenly blue
light. Rejoice in this star with your guardian angel, and receive from
it the blessing of the peaceful breast, rising and falling almost indis-
cernibly with the heart-lit breath.

The Pleiades

It is said that Buddha was born during the rising of the Pleiades,
and that Atlantis sank during its setting, at the time of its midnight
culmination on 17 November. Called the Silver Apples of the Sky,
the Seven Sisters, the Begetters, the Great Spirit, the Seven Doves,
they glitter in the great constellation of Taurus with a subtle,
remote, elvishly dancing fire, silvery and mysterious.

They have always been associated with water, with the bringing
of rain, the renewal of life, and with floods and inundation. A poet's
inspiration says that these seven daughters of Atlas, who are also
said to be the seven daughters of the ocean nymph Pleione, are the
seven dispensations of water: that Alcyone controls the seas and
the tides, that Electra is mistress of flood, that Taygete, Merope, and
Celaeno dispense rains and augment rivers and feed the wellsprings,
that Sterope is in our tears, and that Maia's breath falls in dew,
called in many traditions 'the sweat of the stars'.

Hailed by numerous civilizations throughout the centuries, who
oriented their temples to them and set their calendars and the
timing of their rituals and festivals by them, this cluster of stars,
'that shaking loveliness of purest light', have always announced the
mystery of angels and spirit-beings and the otherworld that such
exalted creatures inhabit – the paradise gardens of the soul.

If the Pole Star is linked with the 'Jesus' energy within our heart
chakra, then the Pleiades are linked with the 'Mary Magdalene'
scintillation in our heart of hearts, which takes the form of a perfect
rose. From that heart of hearts, where Divine Mother resides, Mary,
in her reflection of her, is sending us energies via the Pleiades so that
that most sacred heart-centre will become universal – every point in

the universe will become the sacred centre, and there will be no more disconnection and remoteness. We therefore receive the most beautiful, fragrant, softly resonant love-energy from the Pleiades. Mary, the mother of the Holy Grail and herself symbolized by the white alabaster jar of healing balm, (a symbol of the loving, Christ-conscious heart), seeks to nourish us with this love, so that we come to understand that all we need for our existence at every level can be found within it, and thus within the starlight in our hearts. The Pleiades (actually hundreds of stars, although only seven are visible) shine through a blue haze, one of the colours that reflect Mary's spirit.

Of course, although we are speaking of 'Mary' and 'Jesus' energies, it is important to realize that each star or constellation under discussion has its own mighty, advanced and noble civilization who direct these energies to us via the soul and the spirit of their home star; and, naturally, the human Mary and Jesus are not the actual Christ-Brigid Being, which is vaster than universes. Nevertheless, they are the perfect vessel for its consciousness, and they are key players in the grand scheme that sends everything good to planet Earth and her humanity.

Two of the telling names for the Pleiades are 'the Virgin stars' and 'the Seven Virgins'. Are these the seven wise virgins, who knew the cosmic secret of keeping their lamps alight? And do they lead us to our own 'wise virginhood', in that we may assume, through their support and help, the supreme state of the perfected soul?

Stand under the night sky, and look for this delicate star cluster (there are times in the year when it is not visible, but this does not prevent us from receiving its divine influences). You will find it twinkling near to the vivid, slightly elongated triangle of Taurus. Ask your guardian angel to place a fragrant pink rose in your heart chakra. Gently contemplate the rose, and pray that you may receive these, sweet, cleansing impulses of love, perfumed as a rose on a warm summer's night. Ask your guardian angel to add the power of its supplication on your behalf, to your prayer. It will help to open the communication lines between you and the Pleiades all the more clearly.

Many esoteric teachers speak of the 'seven seeds of Christ consciousness in the heart' which must spring forth before we can enter the next cycle of our evolution. Are these 'seeds' also seven lamps? And do they have a magical link with the Pleiades? Fiona Macleod says of the Pleiades:

> Still the old wonder, the old reverence for this dim
> cluster, this incalculable congregation of majesty and
> splendour, lives on... for not long ago I heard a tale told
> by a Gaelic storyteller who spoke of the Pleiades as the
> Seven Friends of Christ, and named them newly as
> Love, Purity, Courage, Tenderness, Faith, Joy, and Peace.

Aldebaran

This beautiful star, the 'stellar glory of Taurus', has moved the imagination of countless peoples. It has been called the star of good fortune, the star of 'the golden luck'. It is, truly, the star of the heart's desire. Wish upon this star, but know that your wish will only be granted if your wish is indelibly written on your heart, rather than the passing phantom of your desire-nature! Often, we feel 'heartbroken' if our wishes don't come true, only to look back some months or years later and think to ourselves, 'Well, thank goodness it didn't!' Only our golden wishes, the ones that genuinely will nurture us in their fulfilment, will 'the golden luck' touch with its powers of realization.

From east to west Aldebaran is known as the Follower or the Hound, and, especially, as the Hound of the Pleiades, for it seems to follow the Seven Sisters with a passionate faithfulness. Indeed, Aldebaran does work in conjunction with the Pleiades to gently open and awaken the heart chakra to its birthright of giving and receiving infinite love. Aldebaran's particular work is with the 'mind in the heart', that intelligence of love itself which outshines all other intelligence, and which has been called 'pure reason' by philosophers – the all-seeing eye whose boundless vision is centred in the heart.

The star has a beautiful rosy hue, varying from deep rose to the delicate tint of the lovely wild rose whose bloom heralds the summer, although the star itself is brightest in western skies from January until the vernal equinox. Bards have sung of this star that its 'pale-rose flame lights gloriously the cold forehead of the wintry sky', and that is perhaps the best esoteric description that can be given of Aldebaran. The rose of the heart, the loving heart-intelligence, must indeed bless and shine forth from the brow, the mental centre, so that its cold, wintry aspects – the soul-denying domain of the icy intellect – can be transformed into life-affirming vision.

Just as the Pole Star works with the light in our heart to make effulgent the brow centre, so the mystical rose blooms within its heart of hearts as the kiss of the Divine upon both chakras. Work with Aldebaran as you work with the Pleiades, by gently opening your heart to its glory and wonder of love; but also breathe with your guardian angel as when you receive the blessing of the Pole Star. Breathe in and breathe out the spiritual starlight, and see the rose of love dwelling as Divine Spirit at the heart of the jewel in your heart and on your brow as it takes radiant fire, its veils gently lifted and dissolved by the magic of your star-infused breathing.

Aldebaran is the bright, pinnacle star of the clearly delineated Taurean triangle, flashing and dancing on starlit nights southeast (from the point of view of the northern hemisphere) of the Pleiades. Fiona Macleod says of this star:

> How often I have stood on a winter's night, and watched awhile this small roseate torch burning steadfastly in the unchanging heavens, and thought of its vast journeys, of that eternal, appalling procession through the infinite deeps; how often I have felt the thrill of inexplicable mystery when, watching its silent fire in what appears to be an inexorable fixity,... thrice the outglow of the Pole Star... I recall what science tells us, that it is receding from our system at an all but unparalleled velocity, a backward flight into the unknown at the rate of thirty miles a second.

This 'backward flight' of Aldebaran is perhaps a symbolic indication, not of its desertion, but of the fact that it is taking us with it into the 'infinite deeps' of the unknown. In this respect, the 'Hound' leads the way, and our consciousness itself becomes 'the Follower'.

Vega

Vega is the star of compassion. Compassion is an angelic quality, and it endows us with the magic of a profound sharing in the joys and sorrows of others; not only other human beings, but all sentient beings. The fact that the most compassionate form of diet is followed by 'Vegans' is more than just a linguistic coincidence.

We differentiate between compassion and sympathy, because sympathy does not entirely embrace another's sorrow or joy; and yet, compassion is more than empathy. Empathy is the experience of identifying with someone else's pain or happiness to the point where it is as if we ourselves feel it in its full measure. Compassion moves beyond this. It is not passive, a sentience bounded by the self, but proactive, dynamic. We are *moved* by compassion to protect another from suffering, or to do everything in our power to alleviate that suffering. In doing so, we call upon the inspiration of what lies within us, all our gifts of creativity and response. Nothing in our nature that can give is left untapped.

Is compassion love? Spiritual teachers say that it is not, yet nevertheless, compassion is a mountain stream feeding the still and infinite pool which is love. Both qualities are as one, and both express the active principle, and the principle of perfect stillness, serene silence. As if on the ethereal Lyre, the constellation wherein Vega shines, the fingers of loving compassion sound the vibration which resonates with another as empathy; but then compassion brings forth music from that vibration to soothe and enchant what is experienced as suffering, or to make more poignantly deep what is experienced as joy.

In many cultures, especially that of ancient Greece, Vega was known as 'the harp star', because it resides in the constellation which the wisdom keepers of the earth associated with the mythical seven-stringed lyre of Hermes. This magical lyre, which with its music could enchant the whole cosmos, is the perfect symbol of the attuned chakras, sounding its own lovely melodies within the emanations of the seven rays of creation.

The Vegans love such harmony, and their civilization is profoundly concerned with art and the creative process. They are intimately concerned with the spirit of beauty. That is the spiritual star that they court, which in turn gives its perpetual intrinsicality, like an outflow of rapture, to the Vegan star itself. Their culture is deeply musical, and they are adepts in the art of evoking one's individual 'soul note', which nurtures and awakens the soul to its full potential. Their artistry draws aside what both Eastern and Western mystery teachings of our world refer to as the Three Veils of God – Beauty, Wonder and Silence – to aurically reveal the grand, yet poignant and sweet, symphony of the stars.

The esoteric teacher, Irving Feurst, has given us the following exercise to open our hearts to the gift of compassion that Vega facilitates. We are often afraid of giving forth compassion in case unwarranted advantage should be taken of us, and we are sucked dry by too great a demand on our resources. This exercise frees us from these fears, because it summons to us the memory that, when we give love and compassion, we draw, not from our own limited and personal source which dwells at the level of our personality and psychological structures, but from the wellsprings of eternal spirit, which are ever-replenished and can never run dry. In fact, irrefutable spiritual law dictates that, the more we call on these eternal wellsprings, the more substance they yield. Two minutes at least should be spent on each step of the exercise. I have found that performing the exercise with the guardian angel is especially beneficial.

> Go to the heart, via star-breathing, and find the point of stillness within.
>
> Gently focus on the solar plexus, and ask your angel to help you relax this centre.
>
> Draw your breath easily in and out of your solar plexus to

facilitate this. You may like to visualize your angel's caressing touch on your solar plexus, unknotting the resistance
that can build up in this area, and restoring its rhythm.

Imagine that your angel places a flower in your solar
plexus, and see its petals unfolding. The flower points
upwards towards your crown.

Let the flower vanish.

Now imagine that a tree has taken root in your solar
plexus, growing strongly and rising until its green, leafy
top reaches the very centre of your heart chakra.

Ask your angel to bless the tree.

Now see the top of the tree branching out in every direction until it enfolds the entire heart chakra. Inhale the
beautiful green freshness and cleanliness of the leaves,
and feel the goodness and peace and wellbeing that the
tree has brought to your heart

Thank your angel.

The Vegans invest our trees, crystals, and the stone of Mother Earth,
with their beautiful, singing energy-patterns. Become aware of these
as you walk in nature, and connect your heart with the heart of the
earth. When you stand under the stars to receive Vega's blessing, ask
your angel to attune you, and to cleanse and clear the well-shaft of
your heart, so that you may be filled according to the full measure of
your capacity.

Brigid was anciently known as 'the Woman of Compassion'. As
we develop unconditional love and universal compassion, so do we
develop, from the heart-centre, two exquisite bodies to contain
these impulses, which are part of our light body (the higher astral,
which resonates with our higher soul or soul-temple; the lower astral
body is formed by our more earthly desires and habits, and is actually
cast off to harmlessly disintegrate when we 'die'). These two bodies
gradually become one. Brigid helps us with this process; her celestial
inspiration is fomented by the Vegan energies. See her radiant
golden presence blessing the twin chalices of our love and our

compassion, so that each balances each.

The deeper truth seems to be that we actually have two heart chakras (as we have two crown chakras) which are yet one; and just as the Pole Star has a blue-touched twin, and as the Pleiades shine down upon us through a soft blue haze, so Brigid, the Bride, whose personification on earth was Mary Magdalene, is associated with a divine blueness.

Fiona Macleod's account of her meeting in her early youth with Brigid the Bright, the White and the Golden, also associated this colour with her – the colour of wild hyacinths, and the summer wave. Meeting the child among the wild hyacinths, Brigid stooped and 'lifted blueness out of the flowers, which she threw over me'. Waking from a deep sleep after this incident, Fiona Macleod's profound love of poetry and nature, and her inimitable gift for beautiful prose, was born. It is evident from her work that in her heart the twin chalices of love and compassion, of sorrow and joy, were filled to overflowing by the grace of Brigid, the Woman of Compassion. This unifying grace can be ours when we work with her, and our guardian angel, to receive the inflowing gift of compassion from Vega, the fifth brightest star in the heavens. Brigid particularly blesses our eyes, so that compassion may shine forth from them as a beautiful light of love. The centre that receives her energy for this blessing of the eyes is actually the brow chakra, because our two eyes and our brow centre actually form a pyramid of consciousness through which she works. You may also feel a gentle stimulation of your throat centre, as well as that of the heart, when you open yourself to receive the Vegan inflow.

To find Vega, follow a straight line southwards from Polaris, towards the centre of the heavens. Vega is a summer star, and, with Deneb and Altair, forms the 'Summer Triangle'.

Betelgeuse

We work with Betelgeuse to receive a deeper initiation of love. The influences of Betelgeuse are received by all the higher chakras, but particularly the heart and the throat chakras. Betelgeuse shines in the famous constellation of Orion, which, throughout countless cultures, has always been portrayed as a warrior and a hunter.

It is traditionally known as the Winter-Bringer. The three stars of Orion's studded belt give a further clue to his esoteric dimensions; they are called in many countries 'the Three Marys' (Mary Magdalene, Mary the Virgin, and Mary Jacob, the mother of Mary Magdalene).

Disparate as these names are, they all suggest the role of Orion, and particularly of Betelgeuse, that great flame-coloured giant, glowing with orange and yellow fires; for Betelgeuse, vermilion and auriferous, gives forth emanations that are designed to cast a golden sheen upon the soul, so that we may see her more clearly. In doing so, we may integrate her light more thoroughly with our earthly selves, and feel the quality of the heavenly love her translucency bestows in our ordinary lives.

Although, when the soul is first born as the initial, pristine body of the individuated spark or flame of spirit that has undertaken the task of ensouling itself, it is pure and undefiled, it is important to remember that the soul is, nevertheless, still a body – the first clothing of the spirit in the heavens whose destiny it is to irradiate each of the bodies that forms its garments until even the outermost, coarsest garb (the physical body) is lit from within by an ineffable flame. Being a body, the soul, whose true essence is immaculately transparent, can become darkened by our actions and choices, if these are exceptionally gross or deliberately unjust; and yet this soul-body has within it the potential to wed with the spirit (the 'mystical marriage') and become immortal.

Generally speaking, we do not go so far as to darken our soul, but simply tend to muddy our contact with it, becoming unable to see or to feel it because we are so immersed in the mundane details of our physical and material existence. Betelgeuse sends down a sweetly beautiful ray energy that opens our hearts to receive a deeper, purer love than perhaps we have ever experienced before – an influence which lets us know that we are infinitely loved by the universe, and that our own hearts beat in answering resonance just as profound. We will almost certainly find ourselves responding to life differently, because our sense of justice, beauty, truth and joy will be considerably enhanced. We will sense a loveliness and a mystery in life that perhaps had escaped our notice before, and we will love with a spiritual freedom and bounty that will make everything radiant. This is our dawning consciousness of our soul.

If we feel, for any reason, that our soul has become burdened and darkened, we can open up resistlessly to the sweeping, majestic Betelgeuse energies, and allow ourselves to be cleansed by them. The flame in our heart will unite with them to suggest many different ways in which we can cause our soul to admit the radiance of the spirit once more.

Why should the hunter, the warrior, the bringer of winter, suggest the descent of the soul into all its subtler vehicles until it is aligned with the physical body? Many people who can remember 'falling' into the body shortly before birth (it actually takes about 21 years of mortal life for the soul to completely 'touch down', after which time the subtler vehicles gradually become much more concrete and progressively more difficult to keep translucent), or returning to their body after a near-death experience, do not enjoy the experience. They say it is like climbing back into a cold, dark tomb.

Indeed, we do undertake drastic limitation and confinement in order to take up the challenge of earthly experience. The angels have said that they see us as intrepid warriors and hunters, intent on bringing back to the Godhead the greatest treasures, the richest spoils, of creation, won from its very boundaries, where angels fear to tread. They are full of admiration for the human race, because it has undertaken this extremely difficult and risky adventure into matter.

The great aim of this adventure is to wed our spirit-radiant soul with our earthly nature, with our actual body, for then it and the earth will be lifted up into our collective soul-temple, there to experience the mystical wedding and to become immortal. When this is achieved, the physical atoms of our bodies will become spiritualized, and will belong to a world where death and decay hold no dominion.

Such is the great promise of Betelgeuse, and such is the warrior spirit, the spirit of the skilled hunter, that we will need to call upon in our deepest selves to capture and claim our elusive quarry.

Find Betelgeuse by locating the row of three vivid stars that comprise Orion's belt. Betelgeuse is the large bright star which is 'above' and in line with the first, appearing to be the 'lowest', star in Orion's belt.

Ask your guardian angel to prepare you as a receptacle to receive these starry energies, and remember that one of their loveliest aspects is that they enable us, through our guardian angel, to send our love to those who have died, or who may otherwise be far away, so that it beautifully hits its mark. Of course, the implication here is not that people are unable to do this without absorbing the star energies, but rather that our work with our heart chakra and our entire chakra system, with our angel, and with the bountiful largesse of the star blessings, which are given so free-handedly as a loving gift, we can do it so much more easily and fulsomely. The spiritual teacher White Eagle makes this point when he says:

> If men and women would live in close communion with those they love in the in the heaven world, they must create through aspiration the conditions on the earth for the heavenly beings to come to them. You cannot imagine the angels being able to reach humanity in vibrations that are harsh and inharmonious, and where there is broken rhythm: but where there is harmony they can draw very close.

> Spirit is fed by spirit. Your spirit enclosed in your physical body is fed from the heavenly world. *You* must make the effort to cut yourself away from the harshness, the broken rhythm, and the disharmony of a very material world; and so tune your instrument to the higher wavelength, to the harmony of the spheres of heaven.

Rigel

Another of Orion's stars is Rigel, a star of immense proportions that blazes with a dazzling white light and which is the seventh brightest star in the heavens. Working with our heart, throat, and brow chakras, Rigel also harmonizes its energies with the base chakra, and is as the holy dove hovering over the crown centres. It works particularly, however, with our 'unicorn's horn' chakra, for it is here that our link with star-energies is concentrated and amplified, and it is from here that the received dynamics or 'language' from the stars is directed into the heart chakra for transmutation and harmonization. Before gaining an understanding of the chakras or the star blessings, I had always considered (perhaps not so idly, although it seemed so at the time) that Rigel was a perfect name for a unicorn. Something in me had felt the urge to create a fable about a unicorn called Rigel!

We have forgotten how sacred our earth is, how everything physical is a temple, a holy receptacle for divine consciousness. We have cut away earth's and physicality's divine links, because it suits us to ruthlessly objectify everything, and, having thus reduced it to passivity and powerlessness, use it selfishly, for our own ends. The cruelty and ugliness of this attitude is what plagues our civilizations today.

Rigel is feminine or yin in its aspect, and it works with the more masculine or yang human crown centre, which is the unicorn's horn, to balance energies and to do its great work of integrating matter with spirit. Of course, everything that is yin is also yang, and everything that is yang is also yin. Nevertheless, as they manifest at this level of creation as foci where one influence is generally active or outer, and the other passive or inner, these aspects always have to be balanced. Our planetary denial and denigration of the Sacred Feminine has caused a severe imbalance, not only in our earthly energies, but also in our earthly consciousness. Rigel works to heal and to restore this lost balance.

Both the spiritual beings on Betelgeuse and on Rigel have a deep esoteric attunement and connection with water, the soul element.

This gives them the ability to think and to generate their beingness from a holistic centre. For instance, Irving Feurst reports that the masters from Rigel view everything in terms of process, and that their language does not contain the equivalent of nouns, where everything is heavy-handedly separated into objects; so instead of designating a tree as a tree, they would talk of 'treeing'. He also says that they can help earth people to integrate many different dualities.

It is interesting to consider that Rigel might give much-needed aid in healing those who suffer because they are projecting themselves through shattered or split vessels, and have become insane or deranged. The magic of the unicorn, through whose 'horn' we receive these energies, has always been associated with the spiritual peace of the higher worlds. Through Rigel, we can bring that peace, the peace which heals division, right down to an earth that is parched for need of it. Work with your angel when you work with Rigel, and you will see those subtle, starved watercourses surging once more!

Find Rigel by locating the row of three stars that form Orion's belt, and tracing a line 'downwards' from the 'highest' of the three stars to the large, bright star that shines 'beneath' it.

Sirius

In *The Sirius Mystery*, by Robert Temple, an American scholar of Sanskrit and Oriental studies, the tale is told of how two highly esteemed European anthropologists lived with the Dogon people of West Africa for over 20 years, and discovered their unshakeable belief, integral to the organization of their daily lives, that they had originally been civilized by beings who descended from the star system of Sirius. The Dogon called these teachers 'Nommos', and still venerate them as the grand Parent of humankind, the guardians of its spiritual principles, and the monitor of the universe. Their entire religious and cultural structure centred on breathtakingly accurate astronomical data about Sirius and its small, heavy, dense companion (Sirius B), which they saw as providing a centre of stability for the known universe. What the Dogon knew concerning

Sirius was not known to science until the 1920s, or photographed until 1970.

Many mystical texts from ancient and modern times tell us that Sirius has always directly influenced humanity's development on every level, that it actually dispenses to us our evolving consciousness, receiving impulses from supernal realms which it then transmits to us. It works with Betelgeuse and Rigel, with the Pole Star, and with Venus and Saturn. Its great work is with our crown centres, particularly the 'full moon' crown chakra in the middle of the brain. Its symbol, bestowed by ancient Egyptian sages, is a giraffe. The giraffe has no vocal chords, and so is the embodiment of Silence, the mystical secret of the doorway to the spiritual worlds. It also has multifaceted vision, being able to see in all directions without turning its head or its eyes.

There seems to be a strong connection between the earth, Venus, the Pole Star, our sun, and Sirius. The Orb of Sharon, or the Sphere of John, reflects itself through the Pole Star and the sun, but its deeper location might be associated with the heart of Sirius. The ancient Egyptians called this star the Divine Sothis, Queen of Heaven. This appears to be a title for Isis, with whom the star was so entirely identified that it was considered to be her heavenly body – Isis herself. There is a star in the constellation of Argo (the 'first ship') called Canopus, said to be Osiris, whose ever-changing relationship with the star Isis (Sirius), reflected in their conjunctions and aspects, was believed by ancients to create the field of cosmic energy which fed and chanelled dynamics to the civilizations of the earth.

Sirius is the Abode of Angels. The Solar Angels dwell here, dispensing the seven great rays of creation throughout our physical universe. Our guardian angel is overjoyed when we work with it to absorb the Sirius energies, which are so refined as to manifest almost entirely as consciousness. Nommo, the great god of the Dogon people who came down from Sirius to bless them, descended, according to their tradition, on a gigantic arch which spanned heaven and earth. The Dogonese say that 'He' manifests himself in the rainbow, which is referred to by them as 'the Path of the Nommo'.

Within the Sirius energies, then, we see the promise of our mission perfected, for the rainbow is the great sign of Sirius, the perfected 'coat of many colours' that is the soul fittingly clothing Divine Spirit. In Sirius, our chakra quest is consummated. When we open our heart and our higher mind to receive the wondrous play of the Seven Rays throughout our microcosmic being, we become a radiant point in the great living mandala that encompasses creation – the divine rainbow. We become one with the angelic hosts.

Sirius is the Dog Star, the follower of Orion. We have to reverse our negative polarity to receive its unutterable light. Then we realize that it is the God Star.

Sirius gives us the blessing of the stimulation of our Christ Consciousness. Its breath will feed the divine flame in our hearts until it leaps up in glory. It enters our hand as the Sword of Truth, and from then on our abode is the unified heart of Michael and his feminine consort.

Our guardian angel will show us how to wield that sword (endowed with the magical 'word' ['s-word'] to drive back every oppressive and imprisoning impulse that darkens the projection of universal love, universal light.

—◠   ANGELIC SEED-THOUGHT   ◡—

It is the vibration of the angelic life that will help
to restore humanity to its true equilibrium.

BRIGID

Our culture calls the Divine Child, 'Christ', but reference to this great Being or Child of Light exists in all cultures, throughout the ages. (In Islam, it is seen as an angelic being.) We will soon begin to be aware of the Daughter of Light, the feminine aspect of the Son. In our ancient British tradition she was called Brigid the Golden or Brigid the White, Heavenly Daughter of Compassion, Wisdom and Light. In my own life I have always felt the presence of Brigid, the Shepherdess. Bishop Cormac, writing in Britain in the ninth century, said that she was 'a goddess whom the bards worshipped, for very great and noble was her perfection. Her sisters were Brigid, the Woman of Healing, and Brigid, the smith-woman.' Here we see Brigid in her triple aspect, as the Triple Goddess. To me she has always appeared as a golden, flame-like being, expressing the wisdom, strength and divinity of exalted womanhood.

Whilst working on our book, *The Secret Teachings of Mary Magdalene*, Margaret Bailey and I were given the revelation that Brigid is deeply associated with Mary Magdalene – that Mary Magdalene was, indeed, the human representative of Brigid on earth. We were further told that Brigid is most certainly the feminine aspect of the great Christ Being in the heavens, the 'Bride' proclaimed at the end of the Gospel of St John ('The Spirit and the Bride say, Come!'). Jesus and Mary Magdalene formed a complete vessel between them for this great being, the unity of the Spirit and the Bride, to descend to earth and to teach humanity through them. This perfect partnership with 'the King' is stated directly in many ancient hymns of Brigid, as in this Kitchen Blessing (we think that Brigid is definitely a patroness of the 'kitchen' of creation!):

> *My kitchen,*
> *The kitchen of the White God,*
> *A kitchen which my King hath blessed,*
> *A kitchen stocked with butter.*
> *Mary's Son, my friend, come thou*
> *To bless my kitchen.*

Brigid, in myth, is mistress of the Divine Forges, where each soul, throughout the experience of many lives on earth, is hammered into shape to properly house the spark of the Divine that burns within us all.

In a meditation on the Wesak moon recently (13 June 2006), I was given a vision of Brigid/Mary presiding over the task of bringing the angelic essence within the Christ Being (of which she is herself a part) more into focus; building a bridge that can be crossed by human understanding between the human and the angelic facet of this ineffable Being, so that our limited earthly minds might be enabled to better understand the angelic aspect of the Spirit-and-the-Bride that is the Christ. This great Being of Light is the Divine Child, the Daughter-Son of the Mother-Father God. All those who are keen to work with the angelic consciousness and its frequencies at this time in earth's history would do well to attune themselves to this special work of human and angelic fusion that Brigid/Mary is presently carrying out, overlit by Divine Mother, who ultimately has charge of the angels. This fusion does not mean that angels and humans will merge into one another; we are assured that the human path of evolution actually runs parallel to the angelic path. But, although retaining our individual identity, it is the destiny of humankind and angels to unite, and so create an unbroken circle or circuit of brotherhood, for the blessing of the Earth and her peoples, and for the advancement of creation.

In order to do this, Mary Magdalene instructs us to think of the six-pointed star and the perfect form of a rose (of a warm, sunrise pink hue). The six-pointed star is a symbol of Christ, but we are asked to associate it also with the archangel Michael, leader of the angelic hosts. He rules the sun, and blazes with an astonishingly powerful and beautiful white-golden light. His feminine aspect is that aspect of Brigid which is spiritual fire. With inner vision, place the rose within the heart of the star. Focus on this exquisite symbol in meditation, and you will be lifted into communion with the Christ, and with the angelic consciousness coruscating within the Christ-centre.

Brigid was the most deeply venerated goddess of the ancient Celts. Her name, pronounced with a silent 'g' (Bri-ee-t), gave rise to the modern English word 'bright'. She was goddess of fire and the stars, of poetry and artistic inspiration, of music and song, of compassion and women, of purity and love. She was also keeper of the greater destinies, goddess of prophecies and dreams, of the fairy peoples, and of the mystic western isles conceived of in numerous religious traditions. Her emblems are the lamb, the dove, the dandelion (flower of the sun), the rowan tree, with its white blossom and red berries; and the oystercatcher, the seabird that uncovers pearls. In ancient times she was called 'the Shepherdess' by her worshippers.

The famous Celtic mystic, Fiona Macleod, writing at the turn of the nineteenth century, says:

> I believe that though the Reign of Peace may be yet a
> long way off, it is drawing near; and that Who shall save
> us anew shall come divinely as a Woman – but whether
> through mortal birth, or as an immortal breathing on
> our souls, none can yet know.

Who can this be but Mary Magdalene, the personification of Brigid the Bright, the Divine Bride? Born to us 2,000 years ago through mortal birth, she comes to us now indeed as 'an immortal breathing upon our souls'. Fiona Macleod goes on to say, surely as a true prophetess:

> Sometimes I dream of the old prophecy that Christ shall
> come again upon Iona; and of that later prophecy which
> foretells, now as the Bride of Christ, now as the

Daughter of God, now as the Divine Spirit embodied
through mortal birth – the coming of a new Presence
and power; and dream that this may be upon Iona, so
that the little Gaelic island may become as the little
Syrian Bethlehem. But more wise it is to dream, not of
hallowed ground, but of the hallowed gardens of the
soul, wherein She shall appear, white and radiant. Or
that, upon the hills where we are wandered, the
Shepherdess... Brigid the White... shall call us home.

THE SEVEN RAYS

A brief explanation of the seven rays which permeate all creation is given below. It will help you to understand more regarding the colour or colours that your guardian angel manifests. Of course, such information can only be a starting point. Your own intuition, contemplation and meditation on the meaning of the colour of your angel is essential, as is your own inner dialogue with your angel concerning this important subject. It is also likely that your guardian angel will lead you to certain books or articles which discuss the esoteric meaning of colours when you are working with it on this area of study.

The 'eighth ray' is magenta in colour, and speaks of completion, wholeness, an energy system brought to perfection. It gives us a sense of Divine Mother blessing and healing the earth, so that she sounds her own immaculate note in the symphony of creation.

1 Ray of Will or Power. Its colour is red. It is the lawgiver, the ruler, the Will-To-Good.

2 Ray of Love. Its colour is orange. It is the altruistic ray, the ray of philanthropy. We might call it the ray of mother-love. Its love is universal, yet tenderly individual.

3 Ray of Wisdom. Its colour is an intense, beautiful yellow. It manifests as intelligent, creative mental activity arising from the source of the heart, where the deepest intelligence is centred. It is the ray of philosophy, of the illumined thinker.

4 Ray of Harmony. Its colour is green. This is the magical 'heart' of the rays. It gently encompasses and integrates polarities. The spiritual teacher White Eagle calls it 'an expression in form of higher things'. The Holy Grail is a

manifestation of this mystical green ray energy.
Sometimes, the Northern Lights take on the single hue
of this ray, so that the skies swirl with a great dancing
robe of green fire.

5 Ray of Wisdom. Its colour is blue. It is the ray of science,
of the realm of ideas stepping over the bridge that leads
from the abstract to the concrete, from the realm of ideas
to ideation. It includes esoteric, religious and spiritual
science – the science of healing and prayer, for instance,
or the science of archetypes.

6 Ray of Love. Its colour is indigo. It is the ray of the
mystic, of devotion and abstract idealism. We might call
it the ray of fatherly love. White Eagle calls it 'the ray of
true goodness'.

7 Ray of Power. Its colour is violet. It is the spirit of beauty.
Alice Bailey says of this ray, 'The prime cosmic function
of the seventh ray is to perform the magical work of
blending spirit and matter in order to produce the
manifested form through which the life will reveal the
glory of God.' White Eagle teaches that 'The seventh ray
is the ray of Beauty. It brings into operation those powers
which are intensified by beauty, and draws to its
influence or surroundings those great devas which are
present at ceremonies. In this way the seventh ray is
interpreted by some as the ceremonial ray. We will call it,
however, the ray of Beauty, being an aspect of God.'
Ceremony is certainly an exact science, the power and
beauty of which we have largely lost sight of today. The
great ceremonial angels gather and serve humanity and
greater cosmic entities on this ray.

Most colours are a combination of these seven primary colours, and
can be interpreted accordingly. However, there are four which need
clarification.

Gold – solar gold, which initiates, protects, blesses and ignites into life and manifestation. It is the colour of exalted influences.

Silver – the colour of purification and protection from negative aspects of one's own being. It opens the doorway to the astral planes, and is the colour of magnetism, romance, mystery and serenity.

Pearl – the soft play of the light of Divine Mother on the soul. It often indicates the presence of a throng of surrounding angels.

Rose – sweet, nurturing, reassuring love – a manifestation of love and the heart-gift of Divine Mother for our inner child.

THE ENCHANTED
FAIRY ISLE

This guided visualization fosters an awareness of the higher chakras, and the rainbow bridge which, in a sense, is their journey's end – and their journey's beginning. Its length is a challenge. Because of my own tradition, I felt it was necessary that a sacred story about Brigid should incorporate certain crucial components. Also, the task of sculpting an entryway into the fairy worlds is, for me, an undertaking in which I was bound to become profoundly involved. So brevity was not an option! Nevertheless, for the sake of those who might find such a challenge helpful and interesting, it is given here in full.

Before entering the fairy realm, it is vital that we call upon our guardian angel to be with us throughout every step of the way. Of course, the same is true for our journey through our earthly life, and for our travels in the spiritual spheres; but the Land of Faery has its own peculiar perils, which can exacerbate our problems in our physical life if we are so reckless as to take no heed of them. For that reason, when using this guided visualization with those who attend my workshops, I have always ensured that a guide from the realms of Faery is present for every individual who undertakes it. The fairy guide works with, and connects to, our own guardian angel, for fairy life is a natural extension of angelic existence. Therefore, the following visualization offers an opportunity to draw very close to our guardian angel, and to open our deeper self to its presence throughout the imaginal experiences it will give us.

The guardian angel is always waiting to take us deep into the heart of nature, where its fairies and spirits eternally dance in laughter and joy. This might be on a country walk, whilst sitting in the garden, or contemplating an indoor plant, or it might be as we listen to beautiful music or read masterly literature, especially poetry.

I hope that this visualization will particularly help you to experience your guardian angel's opening of the way into the magical worlds of nature that lie hidden beneath our physical perception.

The Enchanted Fairy Isle

Make sure that your spine is straight, fully supported if necessary, and that you are comfortable and relaxed.

You are going to call upon a fairy guide, one of the Handmaidens of Brigid — Goddess of Faery, Woman of Compassion, Healing and the White-Golden Light of the Higher Essence — who will usher you into her holy presence.

Breathe a little more deeply and a little more slowly, 'through the heart', and feel the enhanced magical quality of the airs of Faery as they begin to flow around you.

An enchanted door appears before you. It is arched and made of oak, medieval in design, and studded with gold and silver.

The door swings open. Beyond there is a starry twilit haze.

Begin to hear your guide from afar, singing a song of wild loveliness as she approaches you, a high piping melody brought from the depths of the fairy worlds. Soon she stands before you on the threshold, smiling in greeting. Around her moves a swirl of violet and green mists from the Otherworld.

You are aware, as you greet her, that your own guardian angel stands as a shining presence behind her, ready to escort you, in company with her, through the open door.

You move towards her, out of your earthbound self, and step into the shimmering twilight beyond the oaken door.

Your guide puts her right hand into your left hand, and as you link with her you are given the gift of flight. You surge through the ethers at great speed, aware of stars and spinning worlds and shining mist, as if you were travelling the Milky Way.

You and your guide come to rest upon wide sands which stretch down to a rocky shore, beyond which plunges a northern, blue-grey sea, its passionate waves birthing white horses where the billows become potent towers of jade wine, crashing into the fearful, jubilant body of the ocean with their white steeds of the soul.

All about you is the boom and the joy and the spell of the sea and the song of majestic wheeling flocks of strange seabirds, making music of a deeper weeping ecstasy and a sweeter lamentation than those known on earth.

Before you lies a huge spiral carved into the sands, like the impression left by some some great basking sea-creature. Your guide leads you along its winding path to its sacred centrepoint. As you reach it she lets go of your hand and recedes into a ring of bright light so vivid that at first you cannot register the being at its heart who is casting it. Then the dazzle is gently removed from your vision, and you behold Brigid, Goddess of the human and the fairy worlds.

She is radiant with golden energy, and there is of her something of a wondrous maiden softly clothed in the blue of heaven, and of a tall, fair queen, angelic in her bearing, and of a being more ancient than the stars who scintillates with divine fire. Such is the power of her sublime beauty that sentient creatures can look on her only with adoration and wonder.

Brigid embraces you with her universal love and enfolds you in a cloak of her own golden radiance. She calls you by your name and says to you, 'We will journey together to Hy-Brasail, the Isle of the Blest, the enchanted isle, which some call Tir na Nog.'

You find yourself standing alone again in the centre of the spiral traced on the beach, looking out over the rhythmically turbulent northern sea to the distant horizon.

Suddenly, yet gradually, you become aware that a mysterious island is appearing as if at the rim of the world, at first a blue haze in the faraway, yet growing clearer and more vivid with each breath you take.

So lovely is this island, veiled and remote yet haunting as the presence of a dream, that you walk on to the very edge of the rocky shore where the running waves surge and retreat, as if you would try to walk through the tossing wilderness of the waters to reach it.

On the crest of a wave there bobs into sight a little round coracle which comes to rest at your feet, so small that at first you are wary of stepping into it; but you hear Brigid's sweet voice speaking to your inner ear, and take heart.

'Have no fear. This little boat is built from the charms and incantations of your heart's desire. You have built it well, and it will not fail you.'

You grasp the coracle and jump into it. The next great wave sweeps you away, and you ride on the summit of the waves in exhilaration until you reach the glimmering shores of the fairy isle.

As you disembark, you notice that evening has fallen and that the great sun is making glory on the waves and beginning to sink in a lake of crimson and orange fire below the rim of the western world; Brigid whispers within your heart that you have come to the Isle of the Blest, to Tir na Nog, Land of the Ever Young, and that it is the jewel of the enchanted western isles.

Turning from the splendour of the sunset-bright ocean, you see that that this land is indeed fair and gracious, bathed in a loveliness that never shone over any mortal world.

It is a twilit world of soft dusk and starlight, and you see that it is inhabited by the noble fairies, the Sidhe, who move in shining opalescent garb, weaving magic and influences which they dispense to the dim earth far away.

Their task is a delight to them, and you perceive that they

dance and feast on rare fruits and magical foods drawn from the rays of the quiet starlight all night long under the glittering constellations. Everywhere there are lovers, engaged not in physical conjoinment but in their own created currents of ecstasy, and this in turn is given to the earth, and to other planets which spin in the material cosmos in the remote soul-distance.

You think of the wheeling earth and of the energies of Nature as they are expressed in her verdure, our own green world, and you understand the source of their ardour, the sweet eroticism of their giving-forth. You ponder on these things, knowing they are marvels.

You are approached by a fairy couple strange and majestic in their exquisite pulchritude of form and face and aura. These are the Prince of Tir na Nog and the Mistress of the Realms, a woman powerful and mighty in her faery sphere, graceful as a willow wand.

You know them, you know who they are and that a mutual glad familiarity exists between you even before they greet you. With few words they invite you to join the fairy feasting and dancing.

You are ready to partake of their moonlight revels, and the hours of the night fly by on dancing feet as swift as your own. Once or twice you are guided by the invisible presence of Brigid to look into the bowered glades between the trees, and there in the soft moonbeams you behold the marvellous sight of the kings and queens of Faery, dancing as in a charmed dream with a host of noble unicorns, white as the foam of the wave.

In the morning, the sunrise over the sea is greeted with undimmed delight by the fairy people of the enchanted western isles, because age, weariness and broken dreams cannot approach them. On the Isle of the Blest, in the Land of the Ever Young, you rejoice with them, and receive the unalloyed peace and blessing of the dawn.

After the sunrise celebrations, the Prince of Tir na Nog and the Mistress of the Realms lead you to a natural bower richly festooned with fragrant woodbine and wild roses. They seem full of animation and excitement, as if something magnificent is about to be revealed.

They tell you that Brigid came to them last night in the ceremony of the unicorn-dance and instructed them that you are to be anointed with the Three Fairy Mysteries, called the Jewels of Peace by the fairy peoples of Tir na Nog.

The knowledge comes to you, like a bird flying to its perch in your mind, that the Sidhe, the noble fairy hosts of the inner worlds, are truly the People of Peace, pronounced by ancient lore older than the earth to have the sacred Jewels of Peace in their safekeeping, which they will vouchsafe to heart-centred mortals.

You look deep into your own heart-centre and see there a flame burning, golden-white, ever-radiant, inextinguishable; and as you begin to properly comprehend the profundity of the honour to be bestowed on you, the quintessence of the gift to be given, that seed of light which is the flame within your heart kindles into a star.

You see that it is the nature of a star to perpetually and abundantly give forth its own essence; and the realization comes to you that when you have received the Jewels of Peace, you will be able to continually give of them to others.

The Mistress of the Realms and the Prince of Tir na Nog take you through the woods towards the peak of a Visionary Mountain which glimmers at a spectral distance. As the trees recede you are led to a clear shining lake lying between miniature hills which are clad in a pelt of smooth green grass and moorland flowers. Here, the spirit of the lake, the fairy queen Olwen, rises from the waters to greet you.

Free-hearted, laughing Olwen invites you to bathe in her magical lake, to absorb the beauty of its sweet wildness and loneliness and to wash away the clinging bonds of trivia, superficiality and artificiality of the mundane world which puts the soul to sleep and closes the heart like a sun-deserted flower.

Bathe in Olwen's sanctified lake and feel the descent of soul-calm and spiritual renewal, which make the springing waters of your inner being as limpid and light-filled as the mirroring expanse of Olwen's wild pool.

As the waters wash over you, there comes a sudden rush and beating of wings, and seven white swans fly in formation around the lake. They come to rest upon its shores, and there they shed their swan-garb and enter the water as seven fairy beings, beautiful maidens of brilliant radiance who sport and play in the body of the lake and who yet remain swans but are released from the constrictions of literal form.

Laughingly, they insist that you too have a cloak which shrouds your spirit, and that to receive the first of the Fairy Mysteries, you must be prepared to shed it without shame or regret, as they have shed theirs.

You ponder their words, for you cannot see your cloak. The dullness of earth has washed away from you, but you are not yet a shining being as they are.

As if a spell had stolen over the lake, evening comes, and three constellations appear brightly overhead, twinkling through the dusk.

They are the seven stars of the Great Bear, the constellation of the Little Bear from which the Pole Star shines down with a soft intensity, and the muted fire of the Pleiades, the lovely star-group called the Seven Sisters.

Their reflections dance and shake and stream through the waters, and you know that your soul is earthing their spiritual electricity and absorbing the light-patterns of their supernal currents.

The swan-maidens surround you, and gently remove a shadow which you permit to fall away from your vision.

You see a reflection of yourself in the water, but it quivers and swirls so much that you cannot bring it into lucidity.

Then you see Brigid appear like a sun disc above the swan-maidens. She holds a jewel which is like a cauldron of fire. She anoints your forehead with three drops from Olwen's lake, and places the cauldron into your hands.

Instantly, the reflection stills, and you see that your hands are illuminated by the cauldron of fire, which catches light flowing from an incandescent spinning wheel located in your solar plexus.

'Place the jewel within the wheel,' says Brigid. 'It is the first of the Three Fairy Mysteries, the first of the Jewels of Peace. Your hands are its symbol and its secret. It is the power to serve, your giving of yourself in service. The Jewel is kept bright by self-giving.

'That which is brightest in you must be discovered and must be given, in all circumstances of life. When you give forth the rays of this Jewel which dwells within you, what you give forth will save you. If you do not give forth this radiance within you, then what is within you will destroy you. This is the wisdom and the sacred knowledge belonging to the first Jewel of Peace.'

Wondering, you place the cauldron of spiritual fire into the spinning wheel within your solar plexus, your bodily centre, and fall into a healing, integrating sleep which lasts only for a breath of a moment.

When you awake, you find that the Prince and the Mistress of the Realms have lifted you over the beautiful grass-knolls surrounding Olwen's Lake, and have carried you into a wide, flower-filled valley, above which the sun is in its zenith.

'This is the Place of Rainbows,' they tell you. 'Here you shall prepare for your next initiation.'

In this secluded vale, fragrant with delicate flowers of the wilderness, some shy, some wanton, your childhood self awakens and delights in the golden sunshine and the sweet vivid blue of the heavens, sailed by islands of fair-weather clouds shining with a white angelic purity. At the heart of the valley the Fairy Woman Blodeuedd appears, she who is formed from flowers.

As fair as summer and as many-coloured, she plucks flowers from her own breast and, one by one, holds them in the rays of the sun, so that they express their colours and release their scent through the power of the sunlight as if through a great crystal. She weaves the spell of their individual qualities in a series of healing incantations, so that their magic falls on you as a benediction.

As you receive the virtues of the flowers into your body and into your soul, Blodeuedd gives you the knowledge that there is healing in earthly plants and trees for every human ill, and that healing can be given to a human being not only by ingesting the physical essence of flowers but by absorbing the deeper quintessence of their beauty directly into the soul.

The Fairy Woman Blodeuedd begins to walk to the valley-top, and as she walks she draws a soft veil of gentle summer rain over the green flowering dale. At the head of the valley she turns and creates a living rainbow from the flowers she has used in her spells, and with a further incantation she lifts you up to its highest point, so that you are held in the prism of the rainbow, with its arch sloping before you and behind you down to the valley and, your intuition tells you, deeper still into the dimensions of the physical earth from where you have journeyed.

There you rest, poised in the radiance of your own higher self and in the rays of creation which reach the earth from beyond the firmament. You are borne aloft and supported by the fragrance of the valley of flowers and its feminine spirit, which teaches you to aspire to the eternal peaks of the spiritual realms and to the Invisible Presence which walks there in mystery.

As you rest in the heart of the rainbow, you become aware that it has become a great fountain, and that you are standing in its centre which glows like a jewel, being caressed by the springing water.

The Prince and the Mistress of the Realms are with you, bathing in the rainbow-coloured rays of the fountain.

Again, you watch yourself mirrored in the translucent drops. There you see the fountain springing within you, rising like a rose-tree between your throat, brow and crown, joining the three centres of perception and flowering in a measureless plume above your head. As you observe it, you see that it is a fountain, and flowers, and a tree and a rainbow, and all are consumed and made one in an inconceivable flame of fire.

Brigid appears once more and stands in the fountain with you and your companions. Her golden presence gilds the flashing of the water and makes it dance with the blue of wild hyacinths.

'This is the Fountain of Youth,' she says, 'the three-fold Jewel of Peace and the second of the Fairy Mysteries.' She anoints you with three drops from the fountain, and hands you the golden and silver branch of a living tree, hung with blooms of heaven's light.

'Place this branch within the flame of fire which is the Fountain of Youth inside your being,' she instructs you. 'You can bathe there whenever you need to remember that you are eternally young.'

Brigid touches the hollow of your throat in blessing and speaks again.

'The secret of the branch is that it is from the Tree of Life. It governs your words, so that, in remembering the reality of these spheres of the spirit, you will not speak harshly or hopelessly; for does not your soul perceive here the beauty and nobility of the brotherhood of creation and all its members, and does it not bathe here in the everlasting joy of being, and know that all worlds must culminate in an expression of joy? Nor will you speak with judgement, for you have seen here that dimension gives birth to dimension, and worlds beyond worlds turn in the Creator's heart. Therefore with your words you will seek wisdom, but never judgement, and you shall have peace.'

You feel Brigid's touch in benediction on your brow-centre as she continues.

'What you see and what you hear in your circumscribed earth-world will never make you forget what you have seen and heard in the inner spheres of true reality, and thus you will see and hear differently to those who are enmeshed in materiality. Your eyes and ears will ever look beyond, hear beneath the masquerading illusions which blind and deafen those bound to the mortal world, so that you see and hear always an aura, an echo of deeper beauty, deeper meaning; and you shall have peace.'

Brigid finally places both hands in blessing around your crown centre.

'The light of your perception will draw its breath, its inspiration, from the light you have found within, emanating from the mystery of the spiritual worlds. It will never enclose itself in the darkness of the intellect and the limited human mind. You will not elect to sit in a squalid prison, but will always make journeys and follow quests into dimensions blissfully beyond the heaviness and darkness of the earth-planes. What you perceive will ever dance joyfully in the radiance of your higher vision, and you shall have peace.

'Your words, the windows of your eyes and ears, the doors of your mind, are all blessed, and all shall know peace.'

As Brigid finishes her teaching, you place the golden and silver branch with its flowers of light into the Fountain of Youth you carry within yourself, and fall into a revivifying sleep for a fraction of a moment.

When you awake, you find that you are lying on a bank of soft grass at the very foot of the Visionary Mountain.

A train of noble fairies come riding towards you, led by the Prince of Tir na Nog and the Mistress of the Realms riding side by side. Between them they bring a riderless white horse shining with the beauty of the full moon on snow, its mane like a bridal gown and its hooves shod with the purest silver, full of darting lights.

'This steed is Perillion, prince of the fairy horses of the Tuatha De Danaan,' says the Mistress of the Realms. 'He is for you. Mount, and ride with us!'

You see that Perillion wears a silver saddle. You place your foot in the stirrup and straddle him with ease. On the back of your steed you feel mighty and majestic, valorous and invincible. The wind fills your hair and braces your lungs.

'We will ride to the mountain peak,' says the Prince of Tir na Nog, and at his command the horses rear and prance and bolt up the grassy flanks of the mountain. You ride with the others, in a race with the wind to reach the mystic mountaintop. Perillion's pace and strength is magnificent, and you break through the white mists around the peak and are the first to arrive.

Here it is a different world. There is a stillness and a calm which is deeply magical, and all around you stretch vistas of worlds and spheres and dimensions of unending glory and loveliness.

'This is the beginning of all the worlds, and the world's end,' says the Prince, riding up behind you and looking out with you over the vast star-fields of creation's light. 'Dismount and follow me.'

You follow his instructions and jump to the ground as the Mistress of the Realms rides up and also dismounts.

She walks by your left side, and the Prince walks by your right, as the riders of the Tuatha De Danaan form a great circle around you, still mounted on their steeds.

Under a fruitful hazelnut tree lies the round rim of a well. It is at the topmost point upon the peak of the Visionary Mountain.

You take your place at its edge together with the Prince and the Mistress of the Realms, forming the three points of a triangle around the well-top's ring of stones.

'This is the Well of the Holy Chalice,' says the Mistress of the Realms; and like the answering chimes of a bell the Prince states simply, 'It is the Well at the World's End.'

You look down into the deep, deep well. In here the stars are shining, not reflected but radiating mystical light from their own hallowed and ineffable dimension. Within the well swims a great fish, and you know that it is the Salmon of Wisdom, the oldest creature of all the worlds.

Into the depths of the well the Fairy Hazel, tree of wisdom, of the fire of the stars and the creative flame of the poetic imagination, drops its fruit.

You begin to see Brigid reflected in the waters of the well. As you look into the blue of her wise and timeless eyes, you become the leaping fish, the Salmon of Wisdom.

Hazelnuts rain down into the well from the fruitful tree, and as they touch the water they break open, releasing the kernel within. In leaping joy, you swallow the fruit of the hazelnut tree, and pass into a sublime world where you are alone with Brigid.

'This is the fairy Paradise which lies secretly at the heart of your earth-world,' she says to you. 'It is called the Glen of Precious Stones.'

You look around, marvelling at the mystery of this exquisite place. Surrounding you are breathtaking landscapes, seascapes, starscapes, all formed of the most delicate-hued and spellbindingly beautiful crystals, gems, and jewels; and beyond them, in the distance, rise rock-facets of liquid fire, as if fresh quantities of precious stones were perpetually being birthed into being. Their colours are an ever-flowing, ever-changing mandala of fantastically lovely patterns which rise and fall in eternally new tints and hues, led by a tongue of joyous white flame which seems to be their source and their creator.

'It is the flame of the heart,' Brigid tells you. 'It dwells here, in the heart of Faery which is the heart of the earth-world, and in the heart of every being, and in your heart.

'You can pour the light of the precious crystal which is

your heart into other human hearts, and into the energy-patterns of the many earths that spiral around the one perfect ideation which is the template for all its myriad dimensions; and especially into the earth which is your home.

'This perfect earth must one day be expressed faithfully through all its lesser bodies, even that of your physical earth which is the darkest of all the earth-planes.

'This new age, which will bring a perfected earth into being, cannot come about until the Enlightened Ones, who have received the knowledge of the Three Mysteries, join together and give of their heart-essence, their heart-light, consistently each day, so that gradually a great tide of sacred light will lift your earth into a higher dimension. The breath is magical, and it is through the agency of the breath that the deed is done.'

Brigid teaches you how to simply and naturally breathe forth the sacred light from your heart-centre so that it is given out in love to the spinning earth beyond, and to all its creatures.

She stands by your side, and together you give out the sacred breath, the sacred light, to all the earth.

Give out the light.

Brigid takes you back into the waters of the well, where it seems as if you are floating among the stars. She anoints you with three drops of the well-water, and takes a golden-white six-pointed star from her breast.

'This is the third of the Fairy Mysteries, and the greatest of the Jewels of Peace,' she says to you. 'It is within your own heart already. I hold only its reflection. Nevertheless, place this Jewel in your heart-centre, and always see it clearly in your thoughts.

'Its six rays give out the sacred light, and its seventh ray is its centrepoint, its divine source, which takes the form of a mystical rose.

'The secret of the third Jewel is its power to transform, and its power to give of its highest essence without ever growing less. The more you use it, the more abundant it becomes.'

You place the last Jewel of Peace within your heart, and see it there ablaze with light, enshrining the rose at its centre.

A half-second of sleep steals over you, and when you awake, you are standing at the threshold of the oaken door you first came through, with Brigid at your side. Your fairy guide and your guardian angel wait with her.

Brigid smiles in farewell and, lifting her cupped hands over you, showers you with sparkling spiritual gold. It is her gift and her reward.

Your fairy guide leads you through the arched door, back to your earthly place of meditation. She withdraws into her swirling mists of violet and green, and the door closes and vanishes.

Gently return to normal consciousness, still bathing in the fragrant golden sheen which is Brigid's gift and which clings as softly as flower petals to your aura.

Seal your chakras (crown, brow, throat, heart and solar plexus) with the bright silver cross in a circle of light, and earth yourself if necessary.

Affirm:

The jewels of peace shine out from my heart. I can give their magic to others.

I am clothed in golden shining light. The winds of misfortune and hindrance which blow in the outer world cannot disturb my deep golden dream of peace.

I carry the peace and the magic of the fairy worlds within my heart. Their vital replenishment feeds me whenever the vibrations of the physical world become distorted and discordant.

Thank your guardian angel for its loving protection throughout your inner journeying, and spend some moments in quiet contemplation of its shining presence, ever at your side.

FURTHER READING

Alma Daniel, Timothy Wyllie and Andrew Ramer, *Ask Your Angels: a Practical Guide to Working with Angels to Enrich Your Life*, Piatkus, 1992

Barbara Mark and Trudy Griswold, *Angelspeake: a Guide – How to Talk with Your Angels*, Simon & Schuster, 1995

White Eagle, *Walking with the Angels: a Path of Service*, commentary by Anna Hayward, The White Eagle Publishing Trust (tel. 020 7603 7914), 1998

White Eagle, *The Book of Starlight*, The White Eagle Publishing Trust, 1999

Virginia Essene and Irving Feurst, *Energy Blessings from the Stars: Seven Initiations*, S. E. E. Publishing Company, USA, 1998

Judy Jacka, N. D., *The Vivaxis Connection: Healing Through Earth Energies*, Hampton Roads Publishing Company, INC., 2000